the shutterfly® guide to great digital photos

Jeffrey Housenbold

Dave Johnson

McGraw-Hill/Osborne

New York Chicago San Francisco Lisbon
London Madrid Mexico City Milan New Delhi
San Juan Seoul Singapore Sydney Toronto

The **McGraw·Hill** *Companies*

McGraw-Hill/Osborne
2100 Powell Street, 10th Floor
Emeryville, California 94608
U.S.A.

To arrange bulk purchase discounts for sales promotions, premiums, or fund-raisers, please contact **McGraw-Hill**/Osborne at the above address. For information on translations or book distributors outside the U.S.A., please see the International Contact Information page immediately following the index of this book.

The Shutterfly® Guide to Great Digital Photos

1234567890 CUS CUS 0198765

ISBN 0-07-226166-8

Vice President & Group Publisher	Philip Ruppel
Vice President & Publisher	Jeffrey Krames
Acquisitions Editor	Marjorie McAneny
Project Editor	LeeAnn Pickrell
Acquisitions Coordinator	Agatha Kim
Technical Editor	Bridgette Thomas
Copy Editor	Marcia Baker
Proofreader	Susie Elkind
Indexer	Karin Arrigoni
Composition	ITC
Illustrator	ITC
Series Design	Mickey Galicia
Cover Design	Jeff Weeks

This book was composed with Corel VENTURA™ Publisher.

For my best friend, Saint Ruth. "My heart fills with days of wearing purple, holding hands, and laughing at memories of yesterday and those to yet come."

—Jeffrey Housenbold

For Evan and Marin, my most appreciative audience. "Thanks guys, I'm here all week. Don't forget to tip your server."

—Dave Johnson

About the Authors

With broad experience in e-commerce and building online communities, **Jeffrey Housenbold** possesses a unique insight into how people connect and share with one another online—especially through some of their most prized possessions, their photos.

When Jeffrey was 11-years-old, he received his first camera and was struck with an early passion for taking pictures of family and friends. Today, as President and Chief Executive Officer of Shutterfly, Inc., Jeffrey and his team bring the creative possibilities afforded by digital photography and the online experience to consumers everywhere.

Through the powerful medium of photos, Jeffrey continues to share his family's experiences and memories with friends and loved ones around the world. He lives in the San Francisco Bay Area with his wife and children.

Jeffrey has led numerous consumer Internet companies to success, including eBay, Alta Vista, and Raging Bull, the award-winning community finance portal. He earned his MBA from Harvard Business School and his undergraduate degrees from Carnegie Mellon University.

Dave Johnson is a technology journalist who has been writing about digital photography since the very first digital cameras were sold in the mid-1990s. He writes a weekly electronic newsletter about digital photography for *PC World* magazine and is a former columnist for *Digital Camera* magazine.

In addition, he's the author of three dozen books, including *How to Do Everything with Your Digital Camera, How to Do Everything with MP3 and Digital Music,* and *Robot Invasion: 7 Cool and Easy Robot Projects*. His short story for early readers, *The Wild Cookie,* has been transformed into an interactive storybook on CD-ROM.

In his spare time, Dave plays drums, photographs wildlife—particularly wolves, tigers, and sharks—and is a PADI-certified scuba instructor.

Dave started writing professionally in 1990, before anyone had a chance to talk him out of it. Prior to that, he had a somewhat unfocused career that included flying satellites, driving an ice cream truck, loading bombs onto B-52s in a remote region of Michigan, stocking shelves at a New Jersey Quick Check, teaching rocket science, photographing a rock band, and writing about space penguins. He's still not playing in a psychedelic band, but at least he's found steady work.

Contents at a Glance

Contents

Acknowledgments

Thanks to the online communities I've had the pleasure of helping to build and foster over the past ten years. You've proven that the power of human relationships transcends any physical or virtual medium.

Hats off to the dedicated Shutterfly employees whose tireless work makes my simple role seem trite. A special nod to Bridgette who generally makes me look good and keeps me out of trouble.

To my friends who shoot straight, look me in the eye, and encourage me to enjoy the journey. Though less obvious, a degree of gratitude to all of the naysayers for fueling my desire to prove them wrong.

Lastly, thank you to my three sons, Noah, Aidan, and baby #3, who keep me laughing and remind me of all that is good in the world.

—*Jeffrey Housenbold*

Thanks to all the great folks at McGraw-Hill/Osborne who are always fun to work with—especially Margie McAneny, who suggested this book to me, and Agatha Kim. Bridgette Thomas at Shutterfly was also a wonderfully helpful resource.

Finally, this book couldn't have been completed without an almost continuous dose of the White Stripes throughout the writing process—and frequent breaks to play along on drums. Meg, I'll make a deal with you: if you teach me some drums, I'll teach you to scuba dive. Deal?

—*Dave Johnson*

Introduction

How do we know great photos when we see them? They're the pictures that capture our memories, truly touch our hearts, and freeze special moments in time. We share them with family and friends and want to be sure they last for generations to come. Most important, they put smiles on our faces instantly. Getting those perfect shots, however, is not always easy. And while the technological advances of digital cameras make the act of taking lots of pictures simpler, quantity does not necessarily guarantee quality.

As the father of three young sons and an avid family photographer myself, I know how tough it can be to get the stars to align just right—timing, composition, lighting, and so on—all within a matter of seconds. Upon hearing from many of you who share my predicament, the idea for this book was born. *The Shutterfly Guide to Great Digital Photos* will help you become a better photographer and get more enjoyment from your digital pictures.

So, if you're tired of missing those action shots on the soccer field, or you consider yourself a good photographer but just need some advice on switching from the 35mm world, this book is for you. In these pages, we've set out to explain how to take great photos, use editing tools to improve the look of your images, share your pictures online with friends, and create photo projects for your whole family to enjoy. This book will help you understand how to use the exposure and flash controls on your digital camera, how to transfer photos from the camera to the PC, how to organize and find your digital photos more efficiently, and how to become a master at touching up your images.

My sincere hope is that this book helps you take full advantage of the many benefits of "going digital" so you can create, preserve, and relive a lifetime of invaluable memories with your loved ones.

—*Jeffrey Housenbold*

Chapter 1

Welcome to the Future

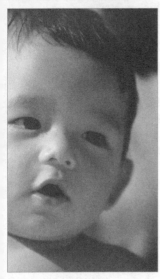

In this chapter you'll learn to…

■ Shop for a digital camera

■ Navigate around your digital camera

■ Pick a camera resolution based on desired print size

■ Choose gear and accessories for a digicam

■ Conserve battery power

■ Tell the difference between a digital and an optical zoom

Welcome to the future. Why is that? Because there's no doubt that digital photography is, for most people and in most situations, the best way to take pictures. It is a technology that keeps getting better and less expensive all the time.

With a digital camera, it's possible to take photos and review them instantly—while they're still stored in the camera—to see if they turned out the way you like. From there, you can transfer them to a computer and easily crop them to size, adjust color and brightness, even perform special effects on them if you want to, and then print the final result to exactly the size you like for a frame in your living room. Then you can take the same picture and share it online with family and friends, transform it into a greeting card or calendar, display it on a TV, or show it to friends from your handheld organizer. The beauty of digital imaging is its immediacy and versatility—just try to do those things with an old 35mm or APS camera.

In this chapter, we'll take a quick look at your camera and digital cameras in general. And if you're still shopping for your camera, flip to the end of this chapter, where we'll tell you what to look for when you head off to make your purchase.

A History Lesson

These days, many digital cameras can compete with the best 35mm Single Lens Reflex cameras (SLRs) in terms of resolution and image quality. Obviously, it hasn't always been this way.

When you consider the first digital cameras that debuted around 1994, it's a miracle that anyone used them at all. The first models you could buy for under a grand included the Kodak DC40, Apple QuickTake 100, and the Casio QV-11. They were strictly for gear-headed early adopters that bought them just to try out the nascent field of digital photography. They certainly weren't particularly useful because they offered poor image quality. That was if you could figure out how to get the images out of the camera and into your PC in the first place.

Those early digital cameras typically had plastic lenses, and the light sensor, the mechanism that captured the image, created horribly fuzzy pictures.

In the early days, VGA resolution (640×480 pixels) established itself as the first real standard size for digital images. Digicams came equipped with sensors capable of capturing 640×480-pixel images, which was ideal for display on a computer screen, posting on web pages, or e-mail, but you couldn't really print such a picture. On a typical inkjet printer, you'd get a photograph that measured just three inches across, too small to be useful.

Then came *megapixel*. "Mega" means million, and "pixel" means picture element or point of color. The term *megapixel* simply refers to a camera's maximum resolution. A megapixel camera can create an image with a million pixels, for example, like 1000×1000 or 860×1200 or any other pixel dimension that multiplies out to about a million dots of color. The first megapixel cameras raised the bar for everyone. No one wanted to own a VGA camera. That started the megapixel race we're still in the midst of today.

Most digital cameras capture anywhere from 2 to 6 megapixels, with a few 8-megapixel cameras tempting photographers as well. Why the fuss over pixels? Well, as we alluded to earlier, the more pixels you have, the sharper your image is and, consequently, the larger it can be printed without getting fuzzy. If you'd like to print a digital photo at 8×10 or larger, for instance, a VGA or 1-megapixel camera simply won't cut it—each pixel would be blown up to the size of a postage stamp to make the picture, creating a blurry mess. Take a look at Figure 1-1. On the left is a detail from a picture taken at 640×480 pixels. On the right is the same detail, but it's cropped from a 3.3-megapixel image. As you can see, the smaller image has fewer pixels to work with, and that's why it looks so grainy. Obviously, you need lots of pixels to print pictures at a large size, and that's why each year we see ever larger-resolution digital cameras hitting store shelves.

The Future of Digital Cameras

These days, the trend for cameras is both bigger and smaller.

Bigger pictures—most folks never make prints larger than about 8×10 inches, and that means a 3- or 4-megapixel camera is good enough for them. But for those folks who consistently want to print larger pictures at home—like 11×17 or 13×19 (well within the capability of some consumer-priced wide-format inkjet printers)—you need more pixels to keep those huge images sharp. So camera manufacturers

FIGURE 1-1   More megapixels means more resolution, which is handy for changing the composition of your picture through cropping, as well as for making good-quality prints.

are responding with cameras that snap 6-, 8-, and even 12-megapixel pictures. These cameras aren't usually very affordable—they clock in between $500 and $1,500—but they're an option for anyone that wants the ultimate in digital photography today.

And cameras are getting smaller. So small, in fact, that most phone companies are selling mobile phones with built-in cameras. This is kinda cool, because you can always take a picture if you have your phone handy. But cameraphones have some serious limitations. Like the early days of digital cameras, cameraphones still take really lousy pictures with low resolution, bad contrast, and washed out colors. This isn't limited to just the cheapest cameraphones—pretty much all cameraphones sold in the U.S. are like that today. Of course, they'll get better. In Japan, cameraphones have as much resolution as some of the best digital cameras and take really good pictures. But that day has yet to dawn here in the U.S.

There's one other trend in digital photography: digital Single Lens Reflex (SLR) cameras. Right now, the most common kind of digicam is the point and shoot model, like the Nikon CoolPix 5400 in Figure 1-2. They look like 35mm point and shoot models, and they automate most of the features needed to take pictures.

But digital SLR cameras are getting more popular all the time. These cameras, like the Canon Digital Rebel and the Nikon D100 in Figure 1-3, don't cost a lot more than top-of-the-line point and shoot cameras did just a few years ago, but they feature interchangeable lenses, powerful flash units, and a wealth of manual controls. In a nutshell, they work and behave just like the best SLRs from the film world. Photographers who love their old 35mm SLRs finally have a digital alternative.

FIGURE 1-2   Point and shoot digicams promise great results without a lot of effort or expense.

If you have a trusty old SLR and want a digital camera that's just like it, this is a good time to be getting into digital. Only a few years ago, the price of these pro-oriented cameras were $5,000 and beyond. Right now, you can find the Canon Digital Rebel for under a thousand dollars!

FIGURE 1-3   SLR-style digital cameras offer a lot of resolution, plus plenty of advanced photographic control.

And prepare for more dramatic price drops in the future. In fact, this table shows how digital camera prices, on average, have plummeted in the past few years:

	Under 1 megapixel	1–2 megapixel	2–3 megapixel	3–4 megapixel	4–5 megapixel	5–6 megapixel
1999	$839	$663				
2000	$716	$461	$885			
2001	$141	$377	$532	$815	$1,733	
2002	$85	$264	$345	$556	$805	$1,982
2003	$71	$193	$310	$477	$725	$1,066
2004	$50	$150	$230	$375	$650	$750

Choosing Your Own Digital Camera

If you haven't yet made your digital camera purchase—or if you are planning to upgrade—you're in luck. The field has never been more crowded with excellent choices, and technology advances keep making these cameras better each year.

Even though the camera field is evolving all the time, the basics really don't change. The next few sections cover the most important elements to consider when shopping for a camera.

Resolution

First and foremost, figure out how much resolution you need. This should be the very first decision you make, because it determines what cameras you will be evaluating. Use this handy little guide to decide what megapixel range you need:

Megapixels	Print Size
1 megapixel	Wallets and 3×5-inch prints
2 megapixel	4×6 and 5×7-inch prints
3 megapixel	8×10-inch prints

Even if you choose a camera with lots of resolution, like a 6-megapixel camera, you can set it to capture lower-resolution images—even a mere 640×480 pixels—making your camera quite versatile. Why would you do that? Well, suppose you are on vacation and your camera's memory card is almost full—but you are taking pictures that you know you're only using to make 4×6-inch prints. In that case, you might want to shoot at a lower resolution so you can hold more pictures than you would normally be able to do at full resolution.

Optics

It is a camera, after all—not a computer. Don't forget that the optics are important. Your camera's optics should be made of glass, not plastic, and multiple "elements" help keep everything in sharp focus through the camera's entire zoom range.

Also consider what kind of pictures you want to take. Having a camera that has a fairly wide angle lens is good for landscapes, indoor shots, and general-purpose photography. If you want to take portraits or wildlife shots, a longer reach is important. But take a look at the specs for a digital camera—what the heck is a 9.3mm lens? Is that wide angle? Who knows? That's why most digital cameras also advertise their focal length in "35mm equivalents"—in other words, if this digital camera were a 35mm camera, its 9.3mm lens would give you the same picture as a 50mm camera, for instance. Many photographers know that 20–35mm is considered wide angle, while 50–90mm is thought to be "normal"—great for portraits, for instance. Anything over 100mm is thought to be "telephoto," good for pulling in distant scenes. 200mm or more is considered a powerful telephoto.

Be sure to check the "35mm equivalent" numbers for an indication of the camera's real value.

Choosing a Zoom

A zoom lens lets you change the focal length of the camera. In simple terms, it lets you choose how much the camera magnifies the image, and zoom lenses let you zoom in and out of a scene for the perfect composition. In general, the greater the zoom the better. You'll commonly see 2×, 3×, and perhaps even 5× optical zooms on digital cameras. With some simple finger pressure, you can use your camera to go from a normal or wide-angle view. The effect of a 4× zoom is apparent in Figure 1-4, taken with the Olympus e-20 at both ends of its zoom range.

Beware, though, of a camera's digital zoom. While optical zooms move the lenses around to magnify the image, a *digital zoom* simply grabs a block of pixels in the middle of the scene and processes them to make the image look bigger. Because the result is grainy and blurry, we suggest that you ignore digital zoom ratings when evaluating a camera and just look at the optical zoom ratings.

Memory

The more memory your camera holds, the more pictures you can take. It sounds simple, but don't forget that cameras come with all different kinds of memory solutions. In general, it really doesn't matter whether your camera uses Compact

FIGURE 1-4 Zoom lenses are popular because of their flexibility when composing pictures.

Flash, SmartMedia, Memory Stick, Secure Digital, or xD memory—the only things to consider are cost and capacity:

- **Capacity** If you only want to carry a single memory card on a long trip and store a huge number of images, a CompactFlash digital camera is your best choice. You can get CompactFlash cards in capacities well beyond 1GB (imagine a thousand images on one card!). Other memory formats top out around 512MB, and the nearly extinct Smart Media card holds just 128MB (not many new cameras have SmartMedia slots anymore, but you may own a camera that uses this format). Of course, you can also buy several memory cards and carry spares, which can be cheaper than buying one really huge card. But, honestly, you might want to just buy a couple of 128MB cards for most shooting situations.

- **Cost** The various memory card formats play a lot of leapfrog when it comes to price, so you might want to shop around for memory cards before you commit to a specific camera. Of course, the newest memory card formats (we're looking at you, xD) cost a bit more than the more established memory cards, like CompactFlash.

Flash

Almost all digital cameras come with a built-in flash. The real issue is how well the flash works. Check to see what the maximum range of the flash is and if it works when the camera is in macro, or close focus, mode. You might also want a flash with special features like these:

- **Red eye reduction**   This mode preflashes the subject to try to minimize reflected light from the pupil, known as *red eye*.

- **Force/fill**   Force or fill flash is used to reduce shadows outdoors or in otherwise adequate lighting when the flash might not fire.

- **Rear curtain flash**   This mode fires at the end of a long exposure. It comes in handy at night so that light trails precede the main subject, illuminated by the flash.

Some cameras also come with sync ports or hot shoes that let you connect more powerful, external flash units.

Special Effects

Because digital cameras are part computer, they can be programmed to do some neat tricks that were inconceivable with traditional film cameras. Few of these effects are necessary; in fact, we'd choose a camera based on solid features like the zoom, lens quality, and overall handling before we looked too hard at whether the camera included a video mode or sepia tint. Nonetheless, these are some of the effects you may see:

- **Movie mode**   Some cameras can capture short, low-resolution video clips, as well as still images. Don't confuse this with real high-quality digital video, though—the results are strictly for web pages.

- **Tint modes**   With special settings, you can take black-and-white or sepia-tinted stills. Remember, though, that you can achieve the same effect in an image editor on the PC after the picture is taken, so you aren't losing anything if your camera lacks this feature. In fact, it's usually better to start with a full-color image; that way you can do whatever you like to it later and always have the high-quality original to fall back on.

Transferring Pictures

Getting images out of your camera is just as important as taking the pictures to begin with.

Of course, most digital cameras use a USB cable to transfer images to the computer. USB is a common, standard cable that connects most external gadgets to computers. But some cameras include even more convenient solutions, like docking stations that "sync" the pictures as soon as you place the camera on the desk.

If you like to view your freshly shot images on a television or want to record them, slide show style, directly to a VCR, then you should definitely consider a camera with a video-out port. Using an ordinary RCA-style composite video cable, you can connect the camera to a TV, VCR, or some other video display unit.

Other cameras include adapters that accept the removable media card and connect to the computer directly. The advantage with these devices is that you can transfer images without draining the camera batteries, and transfers are often easier to do because you drag-and-drop images from a folder on your desktop. Even if your camera doesn't include one of these gadgets, you can add one later. Memory card readers, like the one in the following illustration, let you pop the memory card from your camera into your PC and copy the pictures as if they were stored on a floppy disk. Any electronics or office supply store should have a wide array of removable memory card readers to choose from, and they all tend to cost under $30 or so.

Gear You'll Need

Every hobby has its accessories. Here's a short shopping list of things you might consider buying as you become a more avid photographer:

- **A camera**   It goes without saying that you will want a digital camera, but don't rush into the purchase. You can enjoy the benefits of digital photography even if you use a film camera to begin with, and scan the images into the PC for editing, printing, and sharing. Or, Shutterfly can develop your film, scan your negatives, add them to your Shutterfly account, and deliver the negatives to you. If you've read the previous sections of this chapter and decided what features are important to you, you can shop like a pro.

- **An adequate PC**   Crunching data to process digital images takes a bit more horsepower than you might be used to when working with Word or Excel. These days, a good "digital camera rig" includes at least a 1.5-GHz processor and no less than 256MB of RAM. If you want to work with really big images—like 6-megapixel pictures—then consider 512MB or even 1GB of RAM. You might be surprised to learn that more memory is generally more useful than a faster processor.

■ **Batteries**   Digital cameras are power hogs. If your camera uses AA-style batteries, I highly recommend buying two sets of rechargeable batteries, because they'll pay for themselves before you can say "alkaline." If your camera didn't come with an AC adapter, I suggest that you buy one from the camera vendor's accessories store, so you can power the camera when you're transferring images to the PC or displaying images on a TV. No matter what kind of battery your camera takes, have at least one spare that can be fully charged all the time.

■ **Memory**   Buy the biggest memory card you can afford, or a combination of two cards each with reasonable capacity. The measly 16MB memory card that came with your camera won't last a day when you're on vacation, so having a 256MB, 512MB, or even a gigabyte card is almost essential. A spare card, if it's in the budget, can keep you going when you fill up your main card far away from your PC. (And if you're on a budget, remember that two 512MB cards are usually cheaper than a single 1GB card.)

■ **Image editing software**   Your camera probably came with some rudimentary image editor, but it may not be up to the task. Using Shutterfly, you can easily crop, eliminate red eye, create special color effects, and add creative borders and captions—all for free—so you needn't worry about special software. For added editing capabilities, try a few out, and buy the image editor that you like the best. We like Paint Shop Pro (from www.jasc.com), Adobe Photoshop Elements (www.adobe.com), and Digital Image Suite (www.microsoft.com).

■ **Tripod**   If you want to extend your photography into the world of close-ups or long-range telephoto images, a tripod is a necessity. It needn't be large or heavy, because most digital cameras are significantly lighter than their film camera counterparts.

■ **Camera bag**   Choose a bag that lets you arrange your camera and accessories in a way that they're protected from theft and damage, but easy to use when the time comes to shoot a picture. Look for bags that don't really look like they're holding camera gear—that might make them less of a target by thieves.

How to ...   Choose a Digital Camera

When you're shopping for a digital camera, make a checklist of features and capabilities you want based on these criteria:

- **Resolution**   Decide how large your finished images need to be, and look for cameras that can take pictures in the appropriate "megapixel" range. If you usually want to make 4×6-inch prints, get at least a 2-megapixel camera. Three megapixels is great for 8×10s.

- **Zoom**   The bigger the optical zoom, the more you can enlarge the image. But pay attention to the lowest number of the zoom range, which indicates the wide angle rating, and the biggest number, which is the telephoto setting. And ignore the digital zoom rating, which is more of a marketing gimmick than a useful photo feature.

- **Flash**   Consider the flash range and special features like red eye reduction. For serious flash photography, look for cameras that accept external flash units.

- **Batteries**   Does the camera take standard AA batteries or special Lithium Ion batteries? Does it come with a wall adapter or a battery charger?

- **Memory**   How large is the memory card that comes with your camera? Does the camera also have special internal memory, so you can take a few pictures even if you forget the memory card at home?

- **Picture transfers**   One last issue to consider is how the camera transfers images to the PC—this is a convenience issue. Does it use a standard USB cable? A docking cradle? Does the camera come with a removable memory card reader?

Features, Gadgets, and Goodies

No two digital cameras are the same. Each camera maker is known to some greater or lesser extent for implementing specific kinds of features—like interchangeable lenses, bodies that swivel around the lens, or movie recording features. If you cut through all those goodies, though, you'll find that most cameras share many of the same fundamentals. Let's start at the top and cover your camera's fundamentals.

The Optics

At the heart of every camera, no matter how it stores its images, is an optical system, as you can see in Figure 1-5.

Most digital cameras have two distinct viewfinders—an optical one and a digital one. In most cases, the optical viewfinder is composed of a glass or plastic lens that shows you your subject directly—it's just a plain window that lets you see through the camera to the other side. The digital viewfinder is a large LCD display that reproduces what the camera's image sensor is seeing.

Which one should you use? Whichever one you like. You'll get better results, though, if you understand the difference between the two. With a majority of cameras, you do not see exactly what the camera sees when you look through the optical viewfinder.

Here's why: when taking pictures from a distance, the optical viewfinder and lens see essentially the same thing. Close up to your subject, though, they clearly see two different things (as you can see from Figure 1-6).

The digital viewfinder, on the other hand, shows you exactly what the camera sees and, thus, is the most accurate gauge of your potential photograph. You won't want to use your digital viewfinder all the time, though. For starters, it uses a lot of power, and you can get more mileage out of your camera's batteries by using the optical viewfinder instead. In addition, the LCD display can be very difficult to see in certain lighting conditions, like outside in mid-afternoon.

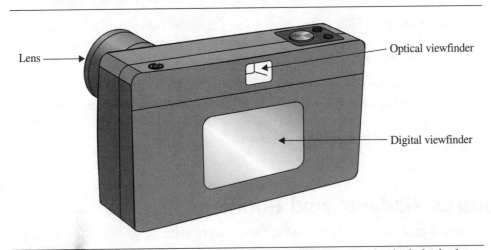

Lens ———→

Optical viewfinder

Digital viewfinder

FIGURE 1-5   Almost all digital cameras rely on an optical system that includes both a viewfinder and an LCD display.

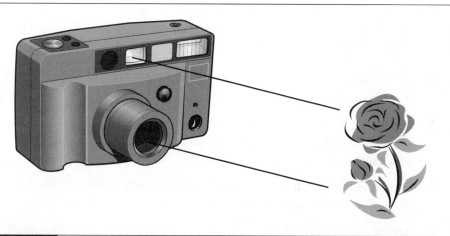

FIGURE 1-6   The optical viewfinder and the camera's lens don't always see exactly the
same thing, especially when close up to the subject.

TIP   *Some cameras let you turn off the LCD display to conserve power. Leave
the display off most of the time to get more battery life.*

Power Systems

Your digital camera, of course, takes batteries. Some digital cameras rely on a standard
set of AA batteries or their rechargeable equivalents.

An increasingly common practice is for manufacturers to design cameras
around special Lithium Ion battery packs. The advantage is that these batteries are
much smaller than a foursome of AAs, so the camera itself can be much smaller.
You can see the size difference between the battery compartments of an Olympus
C-5050 and a FujiFilm F410 in the following:

On the downside, you can't just pop in ubiquitous AA batteries when the cells run dry, which means you need to keep one or more spares on hand. Here's a little advice to help you get the most mileage from your batteries:

- Insert batteries according to the diagram on the camera body—make sure you align the battery's positive and negative ends correctly.

- Don't leave batteries in the camera for an extended period of time. Some kinds of batteries may leak when fully discharged, and if that happens, your camera can be ruined.

- Don't mix and match fresh and used batteries, or batteries of different kinds (like alkaline and rechargeables).

- If your camera takes NiMH batteries, it's a good idea to run them all the way down before recharging them. If you have Li-Ion batteries, though, do just the opposite: charge them more frequently, before they have a chance to fully discharge.

- When you can, run your camera using AC power (a wall outlet) to conserve your batteries for when you really need them.

Some digital cameras come with their own AC adapters, while for others it's an optional accessory. Check the camera body for an AC adapter connector. If you can connect the camera to a wall outlet, especially during image transfers to the PC, you can significantly extend the length of your battery's life.

Taking Care of Batteries

Digital cameras are battery hogs, plain and simple. You shouldn't expect the batteries in a digital camera to last very long because they are responsible for running a number of key functions within the camera:

- The imaging system, including the exposure controls and the zoom lens motor

- The LCD display

- The flash

- Picture storage

That's a lot to expect from a set of batteries, and, in fact, they don't last long—you might typically expect to get between 100 and 200 shots from a set of batteries, depending upon how aggressively you use features like the zoom and LCD display.

Rechargeable Versus Alkaline   If your camera uses typical AA-style batteries, you should avoid alkaline batteries. Instead, invest in one or two sets of NiMH rechargeable batteries. Yes, they're initially more expensive. But they quickly pay for themselves, because you can use rechargeables several hundred times before they stop holding a useful charge. Do the math: Let's say that you use your camera every weekend for a year, and you have to replace the batteries about once a month. Here's how the cost stacks up over the course of a year:

AA Alkaline (like Energizer "Titanium" high-performance batteries)	NiMH Rechargeables (Charger and one set of batteries)
12×$8 = $96	$20

The more you use your camera, the more obvious the savings become. Once you've bought your first set of rechargeable batteries, additional sets are less expensive (usually under $10) because you don't have to buy another charger. So you can see how useful rechargeables are.

Get the Most out of Your Batteries   With so many demands on your camera batteries, it's not all that surprising that they don't last very long. But there are certainly things you can do to extend the life of your batteries, making them

Did you know?

No Battery Lasts Forever

Rechargeable batteries lose a teeny tiny little bit of their life every time you charge them. You can extend the life of these batteries by only recharging them when they're run down; "topping them off" is like a regular recharge in that it heats the chemicals in the battery casing, which slowly reduces the battery's life.

last longer between charges or replacements. Just follow some of these common sense tips:

- **Use the optical viewfinder.**   If your camera lets you, turn off the LCD display and look through the optical finder instead. The LCD screen is one of the biggest energy hogs on your camera, and you can significantly extend the value of your batteries by not using it.

- **Don't review your pictures.**   Likewise, avoid gawking at your pictures on the camera's LCD display. Of course, feel free to review them briefly. But save the slow, careful replays for your computer screen.

- **Disable the flash when you don't need it.**   Sure, there are excellent reasons to use it, even outdoors, but if you are shooting subjects that are 40 feet away and the flash can't possibly help, turn it off. Your batteries will thank you.

- **Leave the camera on.**   If you're taking a lot of pictures in a brief time, don't turn the camera off after each picture. You might think that you're conserving battery life, but, in fact, you're burning energy every time the camera has to power on. That's especially true if your camera has to retract the zoom lens every time it powers down and extend the lens when you turn it on again.

TIP

If your batteries die in the middle of a shoot and you don't have any spares, here's a trick you can try that might give you a few extra shots: turn the camera off, wait a minute, and then turn it back on. Often you can sneak in a few more pictures before the batteries are completely exhausted.

Memory Storage

Memory cards store your digital images for you. The more memory your camera has, the more images it can store. Most cameras includes a memory card with some memory capacity (such as 32MB, 256MB, or 1GB) that, when inserted in the camera, stores images. When it's full, you can remove this card and insert another card for additional storage. Of course, most manufacturers include a pretty small card in the box with the camera, expecting that you will buy one or more additional memory cards for your camera.

Planning to Take Lots of Pictures

How many images can you fit on a memory card? You can use this handy chart
to decide what size memory card—or how many memory cards—to take on
your next family vacation. This chart is just approximate, because the exact
number of pictures you can fit on a memory card depends upon how much
"compression" your camera applies to each picture:

	16MB	32MB	64MB	128MB	256MB
2-megapixel	17	35	71	142	284
3-megapixel	13	26	53	106	213
4-megapixel	8	16	32	64	128
5-megapixel	6	12	25	51	102

   You can use the USB cable that came with your camera to connect and transfer
images to the PC, or use a memory card reader to directly insert a memory card
(see Figure 1-7) to insert the memory into your PC as if it were a floppy disk.

FIGURE 1-7   Five main kinds of memory cards are in use today, and your digital camera
probably accommodates at least one of them. Readers, like the 6-in-1
device shown here, can read your memory card like a floppy disk,
eliminating the need for cables.

Five major kinds of memory cards are in use today:

- Smart Media

- Compact Flash

- Memory Stick (and its big brother, Memory Stick Pro)

- Secure Digital (commonly abbreviated SD, along with its little brother, MMC)

- xD

NOTE   *How many images can you fit on a memory card? It has nothing to do with the type of memory card—all that matters is the resolution of the images and the memory card's total capacity, measured in megabytes or gigabytes.*

Camera Controls

Perhaps the most subjective of digital camera features, the controls are also among the most important because they account for how you interact with your camera. The controls should be comfortable, logical, and convenient. We can't really tell you which is best; you need to experiment with a few cameras to see which you like the best. Try handling cameras in the store whenever you can. Make sure you can reach all the important buttons and try to pick a camera that isn't littered with so many buttons that you'll never remember how they all work.

Digital cameras typically feature two distinct control systems: on-body buttons and dials, plus onscreen menus. Figure 1-8 shows some body controls, such as a *diopter dial* (for adjusting the eyepiece to your personal eyesight), shutter release button, and zoom controls. The onscreen menu (seen in Figure 1-9) is commonly used to adjust less-frequently used controls, like resolution settings, exposure compensation, and special effects filters. That's not always the case, though, as you can see in Figure 1-10. This camera uses a button—the one with the star—to change the resolution without resorting to a menu system.

And don't forget that the best camera in the world is the one you have with you. This means small is usually better than big; even if a somewhat bulky camera seems to have a great assortment of features, a smaller, sleeker model that fits in a purse or pocket might be a better bet.

Eyepiece diopter
control

Optical
viewfinder

Flash control

Menu navigation

Macro mode

LCD display
(digital viewfinder)

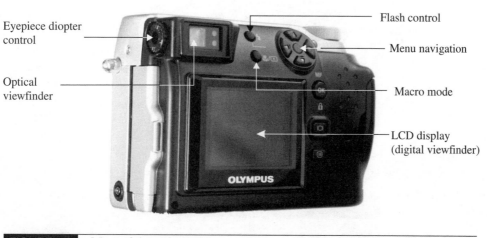

FIGURE 1-8   Most of these controls are common to all digital cameras.

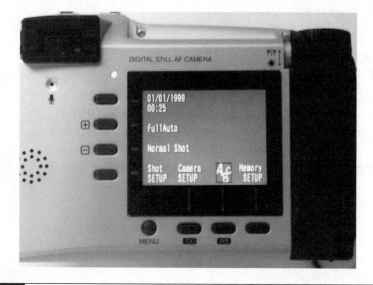

FIGURE 1-9   Digital cameras use a series of menus in the LCD display to operate the
more advanced or less-frequently used features.

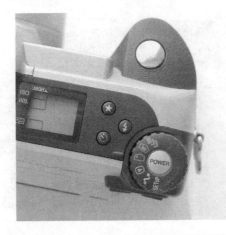

FIGURE 1-10   The star symbol is sometimes used to indicate resolution.

You need to take the time to review your camera manual to find out how to operate all your camera controls. Without knowing how your camera works, you can't really learn to take great pictures.

The Upgrade Race

Do you need to get a new camera next year just because the megapixel bar has been raised—or some other cool new features have surfaced?

No, you don't. Just like your desktop computer, a digital camera isn't obsolete just because a new model came out with more. It's only obsolete when it no longer does what you want it to do. Find a camera you like and stick with it.

Chapter 2

Composition Essentials

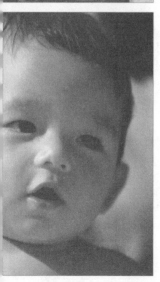

In this chapter you'll learn to…

- ◼ Use the rules of composition to take compelling photos

- ◼ Take less-cluttered snapshots by emphasizing a focal point

- ◼ Take interesting photos with the rule of thirds

- ◼ Avoid cropping out important pixels by filling the frame

- ◼ Use lines and symmetry for artistic images

- ◼ Break the rules for more engaging photos

- ◼ Understand the relationships among shutter, aperture, and depth of field

- ◼ Employ depth of field for pictures that emphasize the subject

- ◼ Zoom a lens to achieve the right field of view

- ◼ Apply rules of composition to common photographic situations

What does it take to make a good photograph? Certainly, it requires more than just knowing how to push the shutter release button. If that were all you needed, we'd all be Ansel Adams. No, taking good pictures demands a little creativity and just a touch of artistry. And the best way to get there is to know the rules of photographic composition.

Composition is all about how you arrange the subjects in a picture and how you translate what is in your mind's eye into a photograph. After all, you and your camera see the world somewhat differently and, to take good photographs, you will probably want to understand those differences.

Believe it or not, taking a picture with a digital camera is not much different than taking a picture with a film camera. That's why we should start by talking about the rules of composition: what they are, how to use them, and how to break them. Only by understanding composition will your images go from snapshots—the ones that get comments like "Oh, that's a picture of your cat!"—to works of art that you'll be proud to frame in your living room.

Why Composition Is Important

Have you ever been on vacation, pulled out your camera upon seeing a picturesque view, but later been somewhat underwhelmed with the final results? If so, you just learned the first rule of photography: reality, as seen by your camera, is quite different from what you see with your own eyes. If you frame all of your pictures without taking that into account, you will always be disappointed.

There are a few reasons why your camera sees things differently. First of all, your eyes are more than just a little camera. Instead, all that you see is supplemented, enhanced, and interpreted by your brain. In a sense, when you see a majestic landscape while hiking through the backwoods of Kauai, some of the splendor of the scene is being added by your mind. Lift the camera to that same view, and you get a totally objective representation of the scene, without any intelligent enhancements.

And, then, there's the fact that a camera has a much more limited range of focus, exposure, and composition than you do. When you look at a scene like the Hawaiian landscape in the previous paragraph, you might think you're seeing a fairly static scene with your eyes. But that's not really the case. In fact, as your eyes dart around, your brain is constantly recomposing the scene, because you can dynamically change the visual "frame" in which you are viewing the scene. Moreover, the dark opening in the center of your eye, called the *pupil,* changes size constantly in response to changing lighting conditions and where you're looking. The result? You don't realize it, but your eyes, working in conjunction with your brain, are creating a visual feast that is difficult, if not impossible, to reproduce in a picture.

In comparison, it's amazing that you can get good pictures at all with a camera. Both film and digital photography have a much narrower exposure range than your eyes. While a scene with lots of sunbeams and shadows might look majestic to the human eye, it would probably be terribly over- or underexposed in a picture. And, unlike the magical pictures in the *Harry Potter* series of books, real photographs cannot change their composition or framing on the fly. What you see in the viewfinder will be your photographic "reality."

What We See

Look around. What do you see? If you look carefully, you'll notice that your *field of vision* is a rectangle with rounded corners—almost a wide oval. In other words, we see the world panoramically. While there are techniques for creating panoramic photographs, most of the time this is not the kind of shot we take.

Nope—our job as photographers is to take the panorama that we see with our own eyes and translate it into an attractive photograph using the rules of photographic composition. As you can see in Figure 2-1, you often have more than one way to frame a picture; it's really your job to decide which works best for the kind of photograph you are trying to achieve.

FIGURE 2-1   Changing the composition of a picture by turning the camera by 90 degrees can completely change the effect a photograph has on its viewer.

Rules of Composition

For a few pages now, we have been alluding to the rules of composition. In truth, they're simple guidelines to help us get the job done and no more rigid than rules of social etiquette. If you violate one, nothing awful usually happens (unless you're still living at home when you violate the laws of etiquette). And that's why we'll be able to break these rules later on—but to begin with, it's helpful to learn to apply them.

Isolate the Focal Point

We know what you're wondering: what is the focal point? The *focal point* is the main subject of your picture, such as a pet or a person. In other words, the focal point is the main point of interest that the viewer's eye is drawn to when looking at your picture.

You should consider what the focal point of your picture is, and then plan your shot accordingly. Photographs taken without a focal point can result in muddy, confused arrangements in which the viewer has nothing specific to look at. Take a look at Figure 2-2, for instance. In this image, there is no real focal point and,

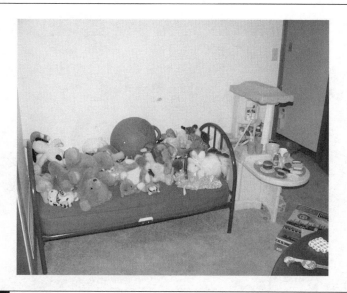

FIGURE 2-2   Without a focal point, your eyes wander the picture aimlessly, looking for something of interest.

thus, there is nothing for the viewer to concentrate on. The photographer should have decided what the subject was, and then rearranged the image to emphasize that. Indeed, most people would think, upon seeing this picture, "Why did the photographer take it?"

When your subject is simply too expansive to be considered a focal point in and of itself, try to contrive a focal point that adds some relief for your viewer. You might try an approach like this when you are photographing a mountainous landscape, for instance. In fact, landscapes really benefit from this approach. A tractor, a mountain cabin, or a gaggle of hikers near the horizon allow the viewer's eyes to rest on something familiar, even though the real subject fills up most of the frame. Technically, this is called a *secondary focal point.* You can see this technique in Figure 2-3, where it gives the viewer a visual resting spot when looking at the backdrop of mountains. The cabin wasn't supposed to be the photo's subject. Instead, the mountains were the subject but, by themselves, they would make a mediocre photograph.

TIP   *As a general rule, try to limit yourself to a single focal point in your photograph. More than one main subject is distracting, and viewers won't know where to look. If you see a photograph in which several objects have equal visual weight, you probably won't like it, even though you may not be sure why.*

FIGURE 2-3   Secondary focal points add interest to landscapes (and many other sorts of pictures).

Use the Rule of Thirds

The *rule of thirds* can help you add balance to photographs and, though this is the second rule we're going to talk about, in many ways it is the single most important rule of photography that you can learn and apply.

Here's what you should do: in your mind, draw two horizontal and two vertical lines through your viewfinder, so that you have divided it into thirds. In other words, your image should be broken into nine zones with four interior corners where the lines intersect. (See Figure 2-4 for an example of this technique.) These corners constitute the "sweet spots" in your picture. If you place something—typically the focal point—in any of these intersections, you'll typically end up with an interesting composition.

This really, really is the golden rule of photography. Thumb through a magazine. Open a photography book. Watch a movie. No matter where you look, you will find that professional photographers follow the rule of thirds about 75 percent of the time. And, while the rule of thirds is very easy to do, you may find that it is somewhat counterintuitive. Many people try to put the focal point of their picture dead smack in the middle of the frame. And trust us—few things in life are more boring than looking at a bunch of pictures in which the subject is always right in the middle. Compare the two images in Figure 2-5. You'll probably agree that the one on the right, in which the subject is not in the center, is the better photograph.

FIGURE 2-4 Every picture has four "sweet spots" to which the eye is naturally drawn.

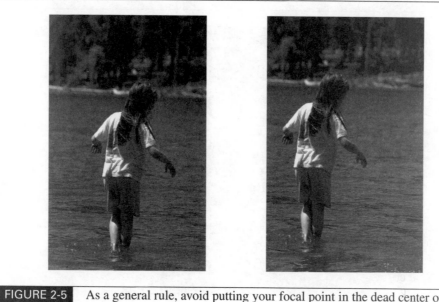

FIGURE 2-5 As a general rule, avoid putting your focal point in the dead center of the photograph.

If you position the subject off-center, the camera may have trouble locking the focus. This is a perfect opportunity to use the focus lock feature on your digital camera. Point the camera at the subject and press the shutter release button halfway down to lock the focus on your subject, and then reposition the camera to compose the picture just the way you like.

Fill the Frame

Don't forget to get the most mileage you can out of the frame in which you're working. What does that mean? Essentially, you should minimize the amount of dead space in a photograph. Once you decide what the focal point of your image is (remember the first rule!), there's no reason to relegate it to a small portion of the picture. Get close. Zoom in. Walk over to it. Whatever you need to do, do it to keep your focal point from being a small part of the overall image. Take a look at Figure 2-6, for instance. In these pictures of the changing of the guard in London, the common wide-angle shots of the event resulted in rather unimpressive photographs. The real star of the show was the guard's face, framed in a very tight shot. Certainly, all of your photographs don't need to be this close. Getting a tight shot of your subject is not always a natural or intuitive thing to do, so you should go out of your way to try this technique whenever you think of it.

FIGURE 2-6   This shot is almost uncomfortably close, and that's why it is so captivating.

The "fill the frame" rule certainly applies in the world of film photography, but it is really important in digital photography, especially if you have a digital camera with just a few megapixels of resolution. If your digital camera only captures small images—like 1 or 2 megapixels—it is important to compose the picture pretty well the first time. There really aren't any pixels to spare in cropping, as you'll need most of them to make a sharp print.

We recommend buying at least a 3-megapixel camera. That's enough resolution for most practical applications—like making 4×6 and 8×10-inch prints. Consider what would happen if you crop your image because the subject was just too small the way the photograph was originally taken. If you crop out half of the pixels in the photo, you'll have a really hard time getting a good-looking 8×10-inch photograph with a much smaller image.

Move the Horizon

This rule is closely related to the rule of thirds. If you follow the rule of thirds to the letter, you probably won't make this mistake, but it is important enough to talk about anyway.

No doubt you have seen photographs in which the photographer placed the horizon right in the middle of the photograph. Actually, the photographer probably did not make a conscious decision to do this—if he or she had, then the horizon probably would have ended up somewhere else.

Running the horizon right through the middle of a photograph is akin to putting the subject smack dab in the middle. It's visually boring because it violates the rule of thirds. Instead, try putting the horizon along a rule-of-thirds line. As you can well imagine, that gives you two choices for where to put the horizon in any given picture. You can put the horizon in the top third or the bottom third of your composition. How do you decide which? It's easy: if you want to emphasize the distant landscape and sky, put the horizon on the lower "third line" in the scene. If you are taking a seascape where you want to emphasize the foreground, such as in Figure 2-7, the horizon belongs in the upper third of the picture. Of course, these are guidelines. Long gone are the days when you printed every photo you snapped, so feel free to experiment!

Use Lines, Symmetry, and Patterns

Photographs are two-dimensional representations of three-dimensional scenes. The question, then, is how to best lead viewers through a picture, so they get a sense of the real depth that the image is trying to depict.

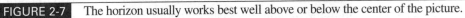
FIGURE 2-7   The horizon usually works best well above or below the center of the picture.

The answer to that question is simpler than you might think. When you compose an image in the viewfinder, look for natural or artificial lines that might lead the viewer's eyes through the photo. These lines can create a sense of depth and perspective that is often lost in the two-dimensional photograph. Lines can be formed in almost any situation: you might see a row of trees, the route of the backyard fence, or the shape of a skyscraper from the ground. Try using the natural flow of a stream or road to lead the eye from one end of the picture to the other. Figure 2-8 is one example of this technique.

While lines like these can fit in with any kind of lens or composition, you may find this works best when seen with your camera lens zoomed out to its wide-angle position. That's because zooming in to telephoto tends to compress your scene and make it harder to see long, sweeping lines.

Another photographer's trick is to look for repetition and patterns, and to incorporate those into your image. Patterns, like those that you see in nature or man-made objects, can create interesting effects. Like lines, they can add a sense of depth to your images. Try combining these patterns with a sense of symmetry.

FIGURE 2-8   A long, straight road is a powerful tool for creating a sense of implied motion in a photograph.

When you employ symmetry, you are balancing both sides of the photograph. That can also help lead the eye through your image.

Keep the Horizon Straight

This may seem obvious, but how many times have you seen a photo in which the horizon was a little cockeyed? Vertically oriented pictures can get by with a slightly off-kilter horizon, but if you take a horizontally oriented image and the horizon is not straight, it affects the feel of the photograph. Try to be as careful as possible while photographing an expansive horizon. But if you goof, remember that with a digital photo, you can always correct the angle of the horizon on your computer.

Use the Foreground to Balance the Background

If you're trying to photograph a distant subject—a landscape or cityscape, for example—a common trick is to place something of interest in the foreground to provide a sense of balance. When done well, the viewer's eyes are drawn immediately to the foreground object, and then they'll wander to the background. This is a very effective technique for adding a sense of depth and perspective to a photograph, as well as giving the foreground a sense of scale. Figure 2-9, for instance, demonstrates this technique.

FIGURE 2-9   The barge in the foreground is the anchor that gives the New York skyline a sense of perspective.

2

Every Picture Tells a Story

Throughout this chapter, and in fact, throughout the book, you'll notice references to "leading the viewer through a picture." What do we mean by that? Often, good photos have a sense of depth and motion or some sort of story. When you look at a good photograph or painting, your eyes naturally start in one place and move to another. Good artists can use techniques like lines, symmetry, patterns, and multiple focal points to lead the viewer in a specific way through an image. If you can create an image like that, consider it a success.

Know When to Break the Rules

Now that we've spent the last few pages telling you what the rules of composition are, we can talk a little about how to ignore them.

Don't get us wrong—we love the rules of composition and think you should follow them. After you become comfortable with concepts like the rule of thirds and filling the frame with the focal point, however, you'll find that you can take even better pictures by bending or breaking those same rules. This is an area of photography that is best experimented with and learned on your own, but here are a few pointers to help you get started:

- **Change your perspective.**   Technically, we're not breaking any rules of composition here, but this is something that few people think about, yet it can have a profound impact on the quality of your photos. Simply put, experiment with different ways to see the same scene. Try taking your picture by holding the camera horizontally, and then see how you might frame the picture by turning the camera vertically. Take a look at the picture in Figure 2-10. Originally, this picture was taken as you see it on the left. Afterwards, the picture was cropped for a horizontal orientation. As it turns out, most people prefer the original framing, but that's okay: experiment and don't be afraid to try something even if no one else thinks it's a good idea. Get low to the ground or stand up on a chair or table to get a higher perspective on the same scene. You have a lot of options: try them.

FIGURE 2-10   Experiment with taking your pictures from many different angles, orientations, and perspectives. After all, you're not paying for the film anymore!

- **Ignore symmetry.**   Sure, symmetry is great. But just as often as symmetry works well in a photograph, you can get an even better image if you intentionally skew the photo to strip out the symmetry. When the viewer expects symmetry and doesn't get it, you have introduced tension and drama into an image. And that's not bad, especially if all you've done is photograph some road, train track, or river.

- **Surprise the viewer.**   If you've seen one landscape or sunset, you've seen them all. That's not really true, but it can sometimes seem that way. Go for the unusual by framing your picture in a totally unexpected way. One handy trick is shooting landscapes through the side view mirror of a car—you can see it in Figure 2-11.

- **Use several focal points.**   While most pictures rely on just one or two focal points, sometimes you need even more, especially when you're shooting a picture like a family portrait. If you're taking a picture with several people in it, you can often overcome a cluttered look by arranging the subjects into a geometric pattern. If the subjects' heads form a triangle shape, for instance, you have introduced order into the photo, despite the fact that a lot of people are in it.

FIGURE 2-11   Successful pictures are often a matter of surprising the viewer.

Using Depth of Field

The last important frontier that you need to understand for proper composition is called depth of field. *Depth of field* refers to the region in your picture that's in sharp focus. When you take a picture, you don't get a paper-thin area of sharp focus in an image; but neither is the entire picture in focus. Instead, there's some distance in front and behind your subject that will also be in focus. This entire region of sharp focus is called the depth of field, or sometimes the depth of focus.

What determines depth of field? Three factors contribute to the depth of field available to you for any picture you plan to take. Let's look at these factors one at a time, and then combine them.

- **Aperture**   The aperture of your lens is the first factor that affects your depth of field. The size of the lens opening determines how much light reaches your camera's *image sensor,* which is the part of the camera that records the picture. Aperture is measured in f/stops, where lower numbers represent bigger openings and higher numbers are smaller openings. While that sounds backward, there's good news: the smaller the aperture's actual opening (or, in other words, the higher the number), the greater the depth of field will be. So just remember this: the smaller the number, the smaller the depth of field. The bigger the number, the greater the depth of field. As you can see here, the aperture setting directly influences how deep the depth of field is in any given picture:

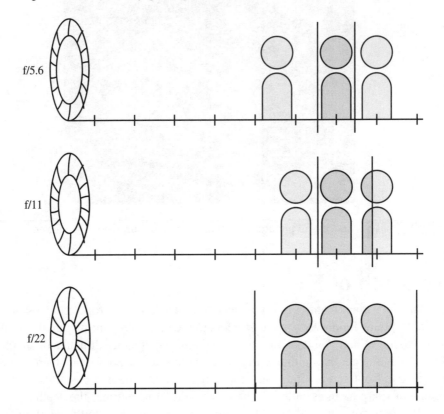

■ **Focal length**   Focal length is just a fancy term that measures your lens's ability to magnify a scene. And, while most people just think about a lens's magnification, depth of field plays an important role here as well. In simple terms, the more you magnify your subject, the less depth of field you have available. When shooting with your lens zoomed out to wide angle, you have a lot of depth of field. If you zoom in to a telephoto magnification, your depth of field drops dramatically. Likewise, *macro* photography (also known as close-up photography) has very little depth of field as well, because you are greatly magnifying a small object. This illustration graphically demonstrates the effect of focal length on depth of field:

2

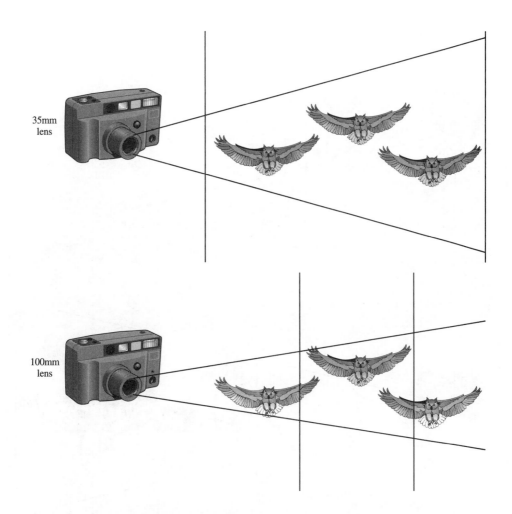

35mm
lens

100mm
lens

■ **Distance**   Last, but not least, your distance from the subject determines
how much depth of field you can get in your scene. If you photograph
a subject that is far away, the depth of field will be much greater than it is
for a subject that is close to the camera. In practical terms, that means the
region of sharp focus for a macro shot—where the subject is only a few
inches from the camera—is extremely narrow, and you need to focus very,
very precisely. If you're photographing something very far away—like
a distant horizon—a vast region in front of and behind the image will be
in sharp focus. Here is what this looks like graphically.

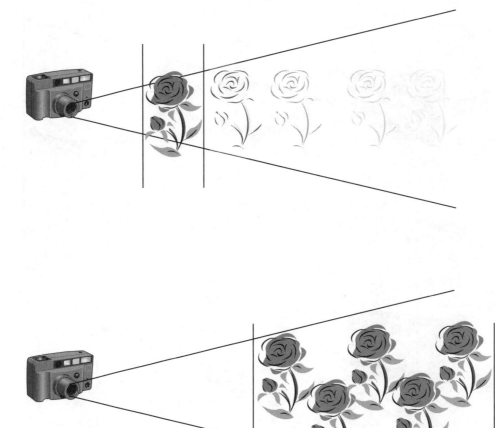

Where the Controls Are

Of course, every camera's controls are a bit different, so we can't show you exactly how to operate yours. But many models are similar. Throughout the book, we use the Canon PowerShot A75, Olympus Stylus A410, and Sony CyberShot DSC-L1 as a guide to using your own camera.

Zooming

Operating your camera's zoom lens is one of the most basic tools at your disposal—and one that's essential to getting a good composition. Thankfully, almost all zoom controls work the same way—as you hold the camera with your right hand, the zoom control usually falls directly under your index finger. The Sony CyberShot DSC-L1 labels the control with both a minus and a *W* for the wide position, and a plus and a *T* for the telephoto:

Canon's PowerShot A75 uses one tree to indicate telephoto and four trees to mean wide angle.

The Olympus Stylus A410 positions the zoom control on the back of the camera, where it's controlled by your thumb, not your index finger.

Control Your Aperture

In this chapter, we talk about how you can change the camera's aperture setting to affect depth of field. Among our three sample cameras, only the Canon PowerShot A75 can do this—turn the control dial to Av, and then push the control dial on the back to the left or right to change the aperture setting, which is displayed on the digital display. Remember that a small number, like F2.8, will give you the smallest depth of field, while a big number, like F8.0, will give you the biggest depth of field with the overall sharpest picture.

Applying Depth of Field to Your Pictures

As you can imagine, these three factors—aperture, depth of field, and subject distance—work together in any shooting situation.

Specifically, suppose you take a picture and your camera picks some particular aperture, say, f/5.6. At a particular distance from your subject, with your lens set to a certain zoom level, that f/stop will yield the same depth of field every single time. But what happens if you change some of these factors? If you get closer to the subject, such as if you walk toward it, or if you increase the focal length by zooming in, the depth of field decreases.

So what is the point of all this? Why do you care about depth of field at all? The answer is that depth of field is an important element in the overall composition of your photographs. Using depth of field, you can isolate your subject by making sure it is the only sharply focused person or object in the frame. Alternately, you can increase depth of field to make the entire image—from foreground to background—as sharp as possible. Figure 2-12 shows the effect of depth of field on a simple portrait; on the left, the child in the background is in sharp focus

FIGURE 2-12   Varying the depth of field changes the look of your whole photo.

Maximizing Depth of Field

You can maximize the depth of field in your image in three ways:

- Use a lens with a short focal length, such as the normal or wide-angle setting on your camera's zoom.

- Focus on a distant subject. If you're trying to get both a nearby tree and a more distant house in focus simultaneously, for instance, focusing on the house, rather than the tree, is more likely to deliver both subjects in focus.

- Use the smallest aperture you can, such as f/11or f/16. This is often the easiest element of your picture to control, and the reason that many digital cameras have an *Aperture Priority* mode for dialing in an aperture setting for your photos. Set your camera to Aperture Priority mode (if it has one) and use the controls on your camera to set the aperture to the biggest number (displayed in the viewfinder).

Not surprisingly, you can minimize the depth of field in a picture by doing exactly the opposite of these things. Pick the depth of field you like the best— a deep depth of field is good for getting everything in focus at once, while a shallow depth of field lets you concentrate on just the subject and not get distracted by a sharp background.

thanks to a deep depth of field. On the right, nothing has changed except the f/stop. By decreasing the f/number (and, thus, increasing the size of the lens opening), the background child is now blurry and indistinct.

Getting the Most Out of Your Zoom Lens

Your digital camera's lens is probably a zoom that lets you change the focal length from a wide-angle or normal perspective all the way through a magnified telephoto. As you may recall, focal length is just a measure of the magnification that the lens provides. A larger focal length produces greater magnification; hence, long focal length lenses are great for capturing objects that are farther away. You can see the effect of a zoom lens on magnification in Figure 2-13.

FIGURE 2-13 These three views, all taken from the same position, show the effect of a zoom lens on the magnification of the subject.

A key fact to remember, however, is that focal length also affects the camera's angle of view. Because a telephoto lens magnifies distant objects, it has a very narrow angle of view. As you reduce the magnification and zoom out toward smaller focal lengths, the angle of view likewise increases. You can see this graphically in Figure 2-14.

2× zoom

FIGURE 2-14 The longer the focal length, the narrower the region that a lens can see.

When you get to the extreme wide angle end of the lens, the image in the viewfinder is shrunk compared to what the human eye sees. The angle of view becomes extreme, sometimes even greater than 180 degrees. This kind of wide-angle lens is known as a *fish-eye lens* due to the peculiar effect of the angle of view.

The focal length of your lens has one other important characteristic. Depending upon whether you have your lens set to wide angle, normal, or telephoto, you'll get a very different depth of field. As you saw previously in this chapter, a telephoto setting yields minimal depth of field, while a wide-angle setting generates a lot of focusing depth. That's why, in highly zoomed pictures, the subject is usually the thing in the picture that's in focus.

TIP

The telephoto end of your zoom lens is great for capturing distant subjects, but the additional magnification can create blurry pictures. Especially if you are photographing in low light, where your camera might choose a slow shutter speed, you might want to steady the camera by leaning against a wall, doorway, or something else that can keep the camera from moving around while you take the picture. Another way to steady the picture: take a deep breath right before you press the shutter release, and hold your breath for the moment that the picture is taken. Then gently exhale after the camera is done.

Chapter 3

Exposure
Essentials

In this chapter you'll learn to...

- ◼ Pick ISO settings for a digital and film camera

- ◼ Match aperture and shutter speed settings for correct exposure

- ◼ Adjust exposure manually

- ◼ Tweak exposure with your camera's EV settings

- ◼ Choose metering modes for better pictures

- ◼ Use exposure lock to optimize exposure

- ◼ Tell when to ignore the camera and make your own exposure decisions

- ◼ Use the rules of composition to take compelling photos

- ◼ Take less cluttered snapshots by emphasizing a focal point

- ◼ Take interesting photos with the rule of thirds

- ◼ Avoid cropping out important pixels by filling the frame

- ◼ Use lines and symmetry for artistic images

- ◼ Break the rules for more engaging photos

- ◼ Understand the relationships among shutter, aperture, and depth of field

- ◼ Employ depth of field for pictures that emphasize the subject

- ◼ Zoom a lens to achieve the right field of view

- ◼ Apply rules of composition to common photographic situations

It seems like some people think that photography is akin to magic. They turn on a camera, snap a picture, and they've somehow got a mystical re-creation of the scene they saw in the viewfinder. How does it work? Who knows?

The problem with the Abe Simpson approach to photography (which Dave has so named based on an episode of *The Simpsons* in which someone took a picture of old Abe and he shouted feebly, "You stole my soul!") is that you can never really improve if you don't know what your camera does or why—and if you don't know how you can influence the camera yourself to improve your shots. This chapter, consequently, walks you through the exposure process. Here you'll learn what constitutes a proper exposure and how to get it yourself—even on cameras that are mostly automatic.

How Cameras Take Pictures

The best place to start is often right at the beginning—how on earth does a camera take a picture, anyway?

All cameras, regardless of type, work more or less the same way. They open their shutter for a brief time, allowing light to enter. The light then interacts with a sensor (like film or a computer chip), and an image is recorded.

Inside a Camera

Traditional 35mm cameras rely on good old-fashioned film instead of an electronic sensor. But what is film, really? *Film* is just a strip of plastic that has been coated with a light-sensitive chemical. The chemical soup on the film is loaded with grains of silver halide. When exposed to light, the silver halide reacts, and that is the essence of photography. The longer the film is exposed to light, the more light the silver absorbs.

The ABCs of Film Speed

As you may know from years of shopping for film, not all canisters of 35mm film are alike. Film is differentiated principally by "speed," represented by something called an ISO number.

The Moment of Exposure

Depending upon the kind of camera you have, the events at the moment of exposure can be rather complicated. In a digital Single Lens Reflex (SLR), like the Canon Digital Rebel, for instance, microprocessor-controlled sensors determine the exact amount of light needed to expose a picture at the moment you press the shutter release. The lens automatically adjusts the size of its opening to admit the correct amount of light. The mirror mechanism that usually lets you look through the viewfinder flips up and out of the way, allowing light to reach the film. Finally, the aperture opens for the programmed amount of time. Most other digital cameras, called point and shoot cameras, don't use mirror mechanisms to let you see through the lens before the shot, so there are fewer moving parts at the moment of exposure.

The *ISO number* indicates how sensitive the film is to light. The lower the number, the less sensitive—requiring long exposures or very bright scenes.

A fairly typical ISO number for ordinary daylight photography is ISO 100. Increasing the ISO to 200 makes the film twice as "fast," doubling the sensitivity of the film. That means it would only take an exposure half as long to capture the same picture; dropping back to an ISO of 50 makes the film slower, halving the sensitivity of the film. As you can guess, 50-speed film requires an exposure (all other things being equal) twice as long as ISO 100. Usually, only professional photographers use ISO 50 film, because it requires a somewhat long exposure (and, therefore, a tripod) even in somewhat bright lighting.

All this has a direct effect on photography. To see why, look at Figure 3-1. This diagram shows a typical camera body as a picture is taken. The lens is equipped with an opening—called an *aperture*—that has a certain diameter and, consequently, allows a certain amount of light through to the film. With ISO 100 film in specific lighting conditions (say, at midday), the shutter might need to open for a 250th of a second (1/250) to adequately expose the picture.

But what happens if we instead try to take the same picture with ISO 200 film? The film is twice as sensitive to light as the previous roll of film. And this means, all other things being equal, that we only need to leave the shutter open for half as long (a 500th of a second, or 1/500) to take the same picture.

That's not all. Suppose you're trying to take a picture in late afternoon—when there isn't as much light available? You might need to leave the shutter open for 1/30 in that situation to gather enough light. That shutter speed is a bit on the slow side, though. Not only might you jiggle the camera as you're taking the picture

FIGURE 3-1   Every camera—no matter if it's film or digital—controls the exposure with some sort of aperture.

(it's hard to hold a camera steady for 1/30), but your subject might move as well, causing a blurry picture. You can probably guess what the solution is—stepping up to ISO 200 film will enable you to grab that picture at a much more reasonable 1/60, and ISO 400 would halve the shutter speed yet again, to a crisp 1/125.

The F/stop Ballet

So far so good—but there's one other thing to consider, and that's the fact that camera lenses can change the diameter of their aperture, thus letting in more or less light as needed.

The size of a camera's aperture at any given moment is called the *f/stop.* F/stops are represented by numbers that start with "f/"—like f/2, f/5.6, and f/11. The larger the number, the smaller the opening, so an f22 is very, very small (not much light gets through to the film), while a lens set to f/1.2 is a huge opening that floods the film with light. Changing the camera setting by a "whole" f/stop doubles or halves the available light, depending upon which way you're going. If you adjust a lens from f/8 to f/11, for instance, you've reduced the light by half.

Of course, there's a relationship among aperture, shutter speed, and your film's ISO rating. Look at Figure 3-2. At a given film speed, you can take a picture with a specific aperture/shutter combination. If you double the film speed without changing the lighting conditions, though, you have to adjust the aperture or shutter speed, so that you still get a properly exposed picture.

So let's apply all this newfound knowledge. Suppose that you want to take a picture of frolicking lions at the zoo near dusk. The aperture is wide open at f/2—it won't open any farther. Nonetheless, your camera needs to use the relatively slow shutter speed of 1/15 second to take the shot. You know the image would be a blurry mess at that sluggish shutter speed, so what can you do? Take a look at your film speed. It's ISO 100. Well, you might be in luck. If you're willing to pop the film out of your camera and put in film that's two f/stops (often, just called "stops") faster, you can keep the aperture at f/2 and change the shutter speed to 1/60. That's probably good enough to get the shot. Just do it quickly—it isn't getting any brighter out, and if you dally, you might find you need to increase the speed by three stops by the time you get the film loaded and ready to go.

Digicams: Same but Different

All that talk about f/stops, shutter speed, and ISO settings may seem irrelevant to your digital camera, but it's not—all cameras use these concepts. The main difference between a digital camera and a film camera, of course, is the fact that digicams

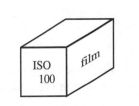

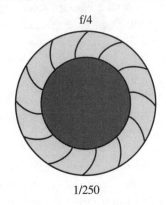

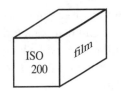

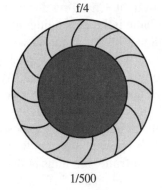

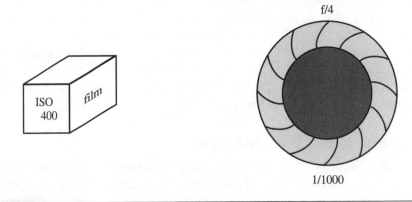

FIGURE 3-2   Film speed, known as ISO, also affects shutter speed and aperture. If one goes up, another must come down to properly expose a picture.

don't use film. That means you never load film with a specific ISO into the camera. So how does the camera work?

Simple. When light enters the camera at the moment of exposure, it doesn't hit light-sensitive film. Instead, the light hits a computer chip, usually called a CCD (though some cameras use a CMOS sensor instead). The sensor is light-sensitive, and each of its many pixels register changes in light. In other words, the silver grains in film and the pixels in a CCD or CMOS sensor are essentially the same thing. They contribute to your picture in the same way, and both are the smallest elements that make up your picture.

The sensor makes a picture by noting the variation in light rays that travel through the camera lens. The CCD or CMOS passes this information on to the camera's microprocessor in the form of varying electrical charges. The image is transformed into digital bits and stored on a memory card.

Your camera's image sensor functions like the film in a 35mm camera, except that it differs in one important way—you can't swap the CCD out of your camera and insert one with more light sensitivity for low-light photography. The sensor is a permanent part of the camera. Camera makers understand that you might need to change the camera's light sensitivity on occasion, though, and that's why many cameras can have their ISO rating "adjusted" on the fly, whenever you want. In essence, what this does is let you "turn up" or "turn down" your camera's sensitivity to light by changing the voltage that's applied across the sensor.

Use ISO for Exposure Control

You can use the ISO control built into your digital camera to vary its sensitivity to light and, thus, mimic the effect of using different kinds of 35mm film. This can come in handy in a number of situations, especially when you're shooting indoors, at night, or in other low-light situations.

But remember not to leave your camera set at the highest ISO all the time. Some folks think that by setting their cameras to the highest sensitivity, they'll be prepared for anything and won't have to muck with the camera menu when they're on the go, trying to take pictures. In reality, boosting your camera's sensitivity to light also increases the amount of digital "noise," or unwanted effects, you're capturing. More ISO means more fringing, artifacts, and digital detritus, as in the following image. Sometimes that's unavoidable, but stick with the lowest ISO value you can get away with most of the time. To do that, set your camera's ISO control to its lowest setting or to Auto, which usually accomplishes the same thing.

Change the ISO Setting

If you find yourself in a situation in which the lighting isn't quite right for your picture, it's time to bump up the camera's ISO value. Remember that most, but not all, cameras come with ISO adjustments, so review your user manual to see if this applies to your particular model. Figure 3-3 shows a typical ISO adjustment; you'll probably find it in the onscreen menu system, displayed in the LCD screen on the back of your camera.

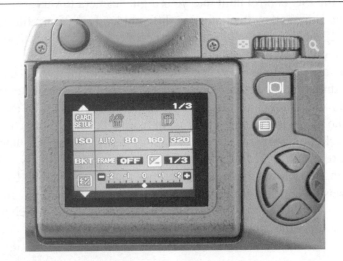

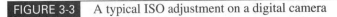

FIGURE 3-3 A typical ISO adjustment on a digital camera

Here are some situations in which you might need to increase the ISO:

■ You're shooting in a low-light situation, such as early evening or indoors. Natural-light photos have a certain appeal, and by increasing the light sensitivity of your camera, you may be able to shoot a picture without using the flash at all. Using natural light can eliminate harsh shadows and produce more natural colors.

■ Your subject is too far away for the flash to have any effect. During the day, you might be outdoors and want to take a picture of something, but there's not quite enough light—such as in winter or during very overcast conditions. Your camera wants to use a flash, but the flash in most digital cameras is only effective up to about ten feet from the camera. So, to properly expose your picture, you need to use "faster film"—that is, increase the camera's ISO setting.

■ You're shooting at night. Most digital cameras have limited capability to take pictures at night or in near total darkness. As a result, if you want to capture anything at all with a night shot, you may need to increase the camera's light sensitivity to maximum.

TIP   *If night photography interests you, investigate what we refer to as "performance" digital cameras—cameras that include manually adjustable shutter speeds and apertures. Using more full-featured cameras with the capability to make long, multisecond exposures lets you get cool stuff like light trails and glowing illuminated signage in your night photography.*

Perfecting Shots with Aperture and Shutter

Let's come back to the idea of aperture and shutter speed. As discussed earlier in this chapter, they're essential ingredients to creating good pictures. Of course, with most digital cameras, you rarely have to worry about setting shutter speed and aperture size at all for typical photography.

How Cameras Choose Aperture and Shutter Speed

Here's what usually happens: when you apply pressure to the camera's shutter release, the camera's microcomputer samples the scene in front of the lens and determines how much light is needed to adequately expose the scene. With most digicams, the camera selects a shutter speed and aperture combination that is sufficient to get the job done. But, you might be wondering, how does it choose? After all, a lot of shutter speed/aperture pairs will work. To take the same properly exposed picture at ISO 100, any of these combinations in Figure 3-4 should be exactly the same.

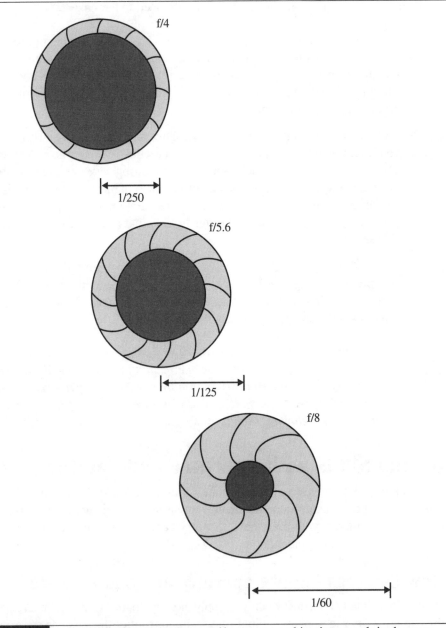

f/4

1/250

f/5.6

1/125

f/8

1/60

FIGURE 3-4   All three of these shutter speed/aperture combinations result in the same overall exposure.

Often, the camera uses the following logic:

The photographer wants to take a picture using the fastest available shutter speed to minimize camera shake and motion blur from objects moving inside the picture.

Although there are some exceptions, most cameras tend to choose the combination that allows for the highest available shutter speed, limited only by how small they can make the aperture, given the current lighting conditions and ISO setting.

This isn't always what you want your camera to do, though, and, in fact, you might sometimes want to choose a slower shutter speed, overexpose the image, underexpose it, or perhaps base the exposure on a completely different part of the picture. That's why you might want to investigate your camera and look for controls that let you tweak the shutter speed and aperture.

Use Shutter or Aperture Priority Adjustments

Instead of relying on an all-automatic system, it's often better to use your camera's shutter or Aperture Priority mode, if it has one. The idea with these controls is that you select either an aperture or a shutter speed, and the camera automatically selects the other half of the exposure for you. This has all the advantages of an automatic system—not only don't you have to think much about the exposure settings, but it also lets you get just the right effect in your photo.

These settings are generally used to find the right balance between freezing (or blurring) motion in a picture and focusing attention on the subject by sharpening (or blurring) the background of an image.

Tricky Lighting Situations

Not all lighting situations are easy to shoot; that's why photography is both an art and a science. It's fairly easy for real-life scenes to trick your camera's exposure sensor and, consequently, under- or overexpose a picture. You can fix that tendency to some degree on the PC afterward (and we'll talk about how to do that in Chapter 6), but it's much better to expose the picture correctly to begin with. That's because an over- or underexposed image is missing information about colors, texture, and detail that can never be restored afterward; only the moment of exposure can ensure that all the information will be in your image.

What are some examples of tricky photos? There are many, but a few problems tend to surface more frequently. Take a look at the second image in the color insert of this book to see what happens if you base your exposure on the wrong part of the picture. If you point the camera at the dark jacket, the rest of the picture will probably be overexposed. Pointing the camera at the girl's face, on the other hand, can result in overall underexposure.

There are several solutions to these kinds of problems, and you can experiment to see which works best for you in various situations. Here are some ways you can correct your exposures when you see a problem in the viewfinder:

- **Use exposure compensation**   Use the Exposure Value (EV) control on your camera to intentionally under- or overexpose your pictures beyond what the camera's exposure sensor recommends.

- **Use exposure lock**   Lock your exposure on a different part of the image, and then recompose the picture and shoot.

Use Exposure Compensation

Most digital cameras come equipped with an exposure compensation control, usually referred to as the EV adjustment. The *EV control* lets you lock in and use the camera's recommended automatic exposure setting, but then adjust that value up or down, based on factors you're aware of, but that the camera may not be smart enough to see. Each Exposure Value (EV) corresponds to changing the exposure by one stop, such as going from 1/60 to 1/30 (this is a change of +1 EV because it doubles the exposure) or 1/15 to 1/30 (this is −1 EV because it reduces the exposure by half).

Take Figure 3-5, for example. In the original picture (on the left), the dark stuffed penguin has confused the camera, making it think the scene was properly

FIGURE 3-5   The EV control lets you use your own judgment about exposure values, instead of relying exclusively on the camera's meter.

exposed when, in fact, it is overexposed. The background and the other animal are nearly invisible as a result. When the camera is set to underexpose the scene by one stop or EV, however, the scene is much better exposed. The image was saved, as you can see on the right side of Figure 3-5.

To use the EV control on your camera, do this:

1. Size up the scene you want to shoot. Decide if it calls for over- or underexposure.

2. If you need to add light to a scene to properly expose it, add exposure by setting the EV control to +1. If you, instead, need to underexpose the scene, set the EV control to −1. Here's a typical digicam display set to EV +2:

3. Take the picture and review the picture in the LCD display. If you don't like the result, adjust the EV and shoot it again.

Most cameras enable you to adjust exposure by up to three EVs, either positive (overexposed) or negative (underexposed). And some models also let you set the EV in increments of one half or one third of an EV at a time for more fine control over your scene.

TIP *You have a digital camera at your disposal, so frame your picture and take the shot. If you don't like the results, take it again with different settings!*

Use Exposure Lock

The exposure lock is one of the handiest tricks you can master. *Exposure lock* is sometimes a part of the shutter release of your camera, but on some models, it's a separate button—check your user manual to be sure. Let's say it's built into your camera's shutter release. Here's what happens when you take a picture:

1. Apply slight pressure to the shutter release button.

2. As you feel it depress slightly, the camera's autofocus lens locks the current subject into sharp focus.

3. At the same time, the camera's exposure meter measures the light and locks in an exposure.

4. Apply more pressure to the shutter release to press it in all the way. The camera then takes the picture and saves it to memory.

The magic of exposure lock is this: as long as you continue applying light pressure to the shutter release, the camera will use that "locked-in" exposure information, regardless of where you later point the camera. You can lock in exposure information for the sky, and then point the camera at your feet and snap the shutter release all the way. You'll take a picture of your feet using the sky's exposure data. You probably wouldn't want to do that because the result will be underexposed, but it gives you an idea of the potential.

TIP   *If your camera has a separate autoexposure lock button somewhere on the camera (usually where your thumb would fall on the right side of the camera body), point the camera where you want to lock exposure settings and press firmly down on the AEL button. Continue to hold the button down while you recompose the photo, and then take the picture by pressing the shutter release.*

Exposure lock is a great tool for telling the camera that you'd like to take a picture with the exposure data from one specific part of the scene. Imagine, for instance, a scene in which you're trying to photograph someone at sunset. The image can be dramatic, but only if exposed properly. We'd like to capture the overall dark tones inherent in a sunset scene, with exciting splashes of color to light up the subject in a subtle way. Just pointing the camera at the scene might result in the camera averaging the bright and dark bits of the picture, generating an image that might as well have been captured at midday. That would be quite ordinary and not at all what we want.

Instead of taking the average picture, here's what you should do, step-by-step:

1. Frame the scene in your viewfinder, so you know what you want to photograph.

2. Before taking the picture, point the camera up into the sky. Include the brightest part of the sky that doesn't also include the sun—that might be overkill. Sounds like guesswork? It is, a little. This is art, not science. You can take the picture, see if you like the result, and reshoot as necessary.

3. Press the shutter release partway to lock in the exposure information. You should sense that the camera has also locked the focus at the same time.

4. Recompose your picture. When you're happy with the scene in the viewfinder, press the shutter release all the way to take the picture.

When to Take Control

Of course, you may often be perfectly satisfied with the results you can get from the automatic exposure controls in your camera. But there will be times when you can do better on your own. Keep your eyes peeled for situations like those described next.

Very Bright Sunlight

Very bright sun can overwhelm your camera, especially if the scene is filled with brightly colored clothing, reflective surfaces, or other tricky subjects. You can reduce the exposure for better effects. Underexpose the scene by EV −1 for starters and see if that helps.

Backlit Subjects

If you are taking a picture of someone or something and the sun is behind the subject, you're usually in trouble—the bright background will cause the camera to underexpose the scene. That means the subject itself will look like it's in shadow. The best way to shoot an outdoor portrait is to put the sun over your shoulder. Nonetheless, if you find the sun behind your subject, overexpose the scene, such as with an EV +1.

> TIP
>
> *If you wear white clothing—it'll essentially turn your entire body into a giant reflector—sometimes letting you put the subject between yourself and the sun.*

Low Light

In low light, such as at night, indoors, or under thick cloud cover, you can often get better results by overexposing the scene slightly, such as with an EV +1. Vary the EV level, depending on how dark the scene is.

How to ... Consider Exposure When Taking a Picture

Most of the time, you can just compose your shot and press the shutter release. But don't forget to adjust the exposure when necessary. Use this decision process:

1. Do I need to adjust the depth of field—that is, make the background more or less sharp compared to the foreground? If your answer is yes, then adjust the aperture/shutter or use the Aperture Priority mode.

2. Do I need to change the shutter speed to depict motion in the picture? If your answer is yes, then again try to adjust the aperture/shutter or, instead, use the Shutter Priority mode.

3. Is the scene significantly brighter or darker than the camera is designed for? If it is, under- or overexpose the scene.

4. Is the subject backlit, such as with the sun behind? Overexpose the scene.

5. Is the subject especially bright, such as on fresh, bright snow? Try underexposing.

6. Do I want to expose the scene based on the lighting in a specific part of the scene? If so, lock in the exposure for that part of the picture and recompose the scene.

Using Your Camera's Various Exposure Modes

Almost every digital camera on the market makes it easy to take quick-and-dirty snapshots using an automatic exposure mode. Automatic exposure is great most of the time, but we hope that you will sometimes want to get a little more creative. And when that happens, you may need to adjust the exposure of your photographs.

Not all cameras offer the same exposure controls, but here's a rundown of the most common ones, and when you would want to use them:

- **Automatic**   In this mode, both shutter speed and aperture settings are selected by the camera to match the current lighting. Some digital camera automatic modes try to select the fastest shutter speed possible to minimize camera shake when you take a picture, while most choose something in the middle: a compromise between speed and depth of field. There's generally nothing you can do to change the settings that the camera chooses when it's set to fully automatic, except for adjusting the EV dial to over- or underexpose the scene.

- **Program**   The Program mode (usually indicated by the letter *P* on your camera's dial or LCD display) is similar to an automatic mode. Although the camera selects both the aperture and shutter, you can generally modify the camera's selection by turning a dial or pressing a button. The effect: you can increase or decrease the shutter speed, and the camera will adjust the aperture to match. This is a good compromise between fully automatic operation and manual selection. Use this mode if you don't want to worry about devising your own exposure values, but you still want some say over the shutter speed or aperture.

TIP   *The Program Exposure mode is often the best all-around setting for your camera. In this mode, the camera chooses a good exposure setting, but you can turn a dial to tweak the shutter speed. The camera will instantly compensate by changing the aperture setting, keeping the overall exposure the same.*

- **Scene**   Many digital cameras come with a handful of Scene modes with names like Night, Portrait, Sand & Snow, Sports, and Landscape. Select the scene name that best represents the kind of picture you're trying to take, and the camera will automatically set the depth of field, exposure, and other factors to give you a good picture. Sports mode sets the shutter speed very high, for instance, while Sand & Snow compensates for the very bright background, which would otherwise underexpose your photo. When used appropriately, these Scene modes work great and let you properly expose a wide variety of settings with little effort. Cameras with just a few scene selections may place the icons on the body (such as on a control dial, see the following), while cameras with many scene selections tend to place them in the onscreen menu.

- **Shutter priority**   This setting is usually indicated by the letter *S* on your camera's mode dial or LCD display. Using this mode, you can dial in whatever shutter speed you like, and the camera accommodates by setting the appropriate aperture to match. This mode is ideal for locking in a speed fast enough to freeze action scenes, or slow enough to intentionally blur motion.

- **Aperture priority**   This setting is usually indicated by the letter *A* on your mode dial or LCD display. Using this mode, you can dial in the aperture setting you like, and the camera accommodates by setting the appropriate shutter speed. Use this mode if you are trying to achieve a particular depth of field and you don't care about the shutter speed.

- **Manual**   The Manual mode (typically indicated with an *M*) is like a traditional noncomputerized camera. In Manual mode, you select the aperture and shutter speed on your own, sometimes with the help of the camera's recommendation. This mode is best used for long exposures or other special situations when the camera's meter is not reliable.

Choosing Exposure Modes and Lenses in Special Situations

Now that you know what your camera's various exposure modes are for, you can think about using them when you encounter unique photographic situations. Every situation is a little bit different, but here are a few general guidelines that can get you started.

Portrait Photography

Taking pictures of people can be fun but intimidating. It's hard to get a natural pose from people when they know they are being photographed.

Where the Controls Are

Of course, every camera's controls are a bit different, so we can't show you exactly how to operate yours. But many models are similar. Throughout this book, we use the Canon PowerShot A75, Olympus Stylus A410, and Sony CyberShot DSC-L1 as a guide to using your own camera.

Pick an Exposure Mode

Nearly all digital cameras come with a handful of exposure modes optimized for all sorts of situations—you just have to know how to get to them. On the *Canon PowerShot A75*, your starting point is the control dial on top of the camera. The *P*, *Tv*, *Av*, and *M* stand for Program, Shutter Priority, Aperture Priority, and Manual modes, respectively. But you can also pick icons for Twilight, Sports, Portrait mode, and others. To get to some of the less-common modes, like Fireworks, Underwater, and Beach or Snow, choose SCN from the dial, and use the left and right arrow keys to pick the right mode from the digital display.

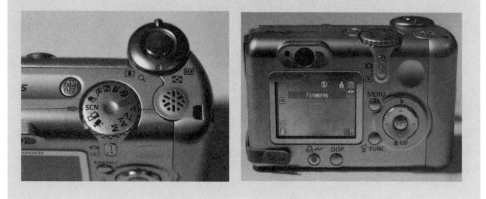

On the *Sony DSC-L1*, press the menu button and arrow over to the Camera menu on the digital display. Then arrow up or down to choose from among the half-dozen or so programmed scenes.

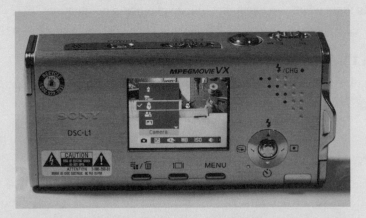

If you have a camera like the *Olympus Stylus A410*, press the top button (with the ring icon) to see the "ring" of exposure modes on the digital display. Then spin the ring with the left and right arrows until you get the mode you want to use.

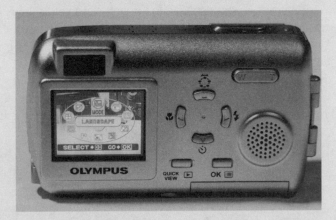

Change the ISO

Increasing the ISO setting can make your camera more sensitive to light, which helps take better pictures in low light. Some cameras, like the *Olympus Stylus A410*, have a fixed ISO setting, but many models let you tweak the setting.

On the *Canon PowerShot A75*, you need to be in Program, Aperture Priority, Shutter Priority, or Manual mode; you can't change ISO in Auto or any of the preset modes. Then press the FUNC button on the back of the camera and press the down arrow until ISO is selected on the digital display on the back of the camera. Finally, use the right arrow to increase the ISO to 100, 200, or 400, and then press FUNC again to keep this setting.

3

On the *Sony CyberShot DSC-L1*, press the menu button, and then nudge the control button to the left or right until you see the ISO menu. Move the control button up until you've selected 200 or 400, and then press menu to save your changes.

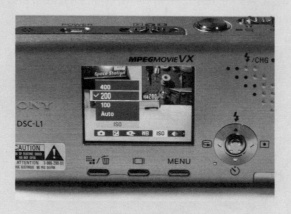

Use Exposure Compensation

Another handy trick is exposure compensation—with many cameras, you can intentionally over- or underexpose a picture if the camera's exposure system isn't quite getting things right.

On the *Canon PowerShot A75*, press the FUNC button on the back of the camera. The exposure compensation control is the first item at the top of the menu. Use the right and left arrows to set the desired amount of compensation, and then press FUNC again to keep this setting.

On the *Sony CyberShot DSC-L1*, press the menu button, and then push the control button to the left or right until you see the EV menu. Move the control button up or down to set the desired exposure compensation, and then press menu to save your changes.

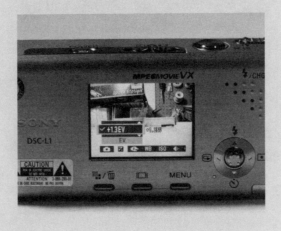

3

The best way to capture good portraits is to work with your subjects so they are a little more at ease. If you're trying to capture spontaneous, candid moments, then back off and try to blend in with the background. If you're trying to capture a fairly formal-looking portrait, you have a little more work cut out for you. It's up to you as the photographer to put your subjects at ease. Talk to your subjects and get them to respond. If you can get them to loosen up, they'll exhibit more natural responses and look better on film. Take pictures periodically as you pose your subjects to get them used to the shutter going off, even if it isn't a picture you intend to keep.

Digital cameras have a cool advantage for portraiture that SLRs don't: the LCD display lets you put your subject more at ease. Try framing your picture using the LCD display, keeping the camera some distance away from your face. That leaves you free to interact with your subject without having an intimidating camera obscuring your face.

The best way to capture portraits is typically with the medium telephoto lens: in the 35mm world, that would be about 100mm. For a typical digital camera, that's near the maximum magnification for your zoom lens. It's a good idea to work in Aperture Priority mode if possible. Aperture Priority mode will let you change the depth of field quickly and easily as you frame your images. Specifically, good portraits have very shallow depth of field. You want to draw attention to the subject of your picture, and leave the background an indistinct blur. Figure 3-6, for instance, demonstrates shallow depth of field in a fairly candid portrait.

 FIGURE 3-6 Portraits tend to work best with a moderate telephoto magnification and low f/numbers.

You can't see the effect of aperture on depth of field in the optical viewfinder, but the LCD display can show you the depth of field. To see, press the shutter release halfway down. That locks in the focus and triggers the aperture to close to the proper position for the impending picture. Now—with the shutter halfway depressed—you can see the depth of field in your picture. Even so, depth of field can be a hard thing to see, especially on an LCD display in bright daylight.

Action Photography

Action photography is often considered the most exciting kind of photography, but it's also the most demanding for both your technique and your equipment. As in all kinds of photography, you can no doubt take some great pictures with anything from a wide-angle lens all the way up to the photographic equivalent of the Hubble telescope. And wide-angle lenses do, in fact, have a role in action photography. But the essence of many action shots is a highly magnified immediacy—something you can only get with the telephoto lens.

The shutter priority setting on your digital camera was born for action photography. To freeze action, you'll need to use a fairly fast shutter speed. Luckily, this higher shutter speed works to your advantage by opening the aperture and diminishing the depth of field; this draws the viewer's attention specifically to your subject. On the downside, of course, focusing is more critical because the depth of field is more shallow.

Nature and Landscapes

Unlike action photography and portraiture that rely on telephoto lenses to compress the action into an intimate experience, landscapes typically work best with wide-angle lenses that let you include huge, expansive swaths of land, air, and sea in a single frame. Zoom out for best results most of the time, and adjust the camera's exposure in Aperture Priority mode (if possible) to get deep or shallow depth of field, depending upon what works best for the picture in question.

Chapter 4

Sports, Action, and Active Kids

In this chapter you'll learn to...

- Catch fast-moving subjects despite shutter lag
- Stop the action with shutter and sports modes
- Pan for action
- Freeze kids at sporting events
- Take beautiful waterfall pictures
- Capture wildlife at the zoo and in the woods

Everybody likes motion—even our vocabulary makes that clear. We love "movers and shakers," for instance. We describe fun friends as having animated personalities; the good stuff is always up and coming. Slowpokes, like sloths and snails, on the other hand, have a somewhat less glowing reputation. So, if motion is such a good thing, perhaps we should put a little in our photographs.

But you already know that. Action photography—like shooting sporting events and kids, well, pretty much doing anything—are some of the most common photographic subjects. And so you know just how tricky it can be to catch a picture of your kid running around the bases of a softball game. In this chapter, you see how to capture sports, action, and kid photography.

Action Photography Essentials

Action photography is often considered the most exciting kind of photography, but it's also the most demanding. The problem—obviously—is that you're taking pictures of things that are moving. And that means not only do you need a shutter speed fast enough to "stop the action," but you also have to contend with the slight delay between when you press the shutter speed and when the picture gets taken—this is called *shutter lag,* and it's common to many digital cameras. Let's talk lag first.

Avoiding the Dreaded Lag

Often, the most common complaint we hear about digital cameras is this: "There's a long pause between when I press the shutter release and when the picture is taken." The result: when trying to take an action shot, the subject sometimes moves before you can take the picture. You may see the picture on the left in the viewfinder, but what you get on your memory card is the picture on the right:

How to ...   **Capture the Moment**

Most digital cameras have a two-step shutter release. Knowing how to use it is key to taking great pictures.

When you put a little pressure on the shutter release button, the camera springs into action—it locks in the focus. If you continue to hold down the shutter button, the focus won't change; you can then recompose the picture and, when it meets your approval, press the shutter release all the way to take the picture.

You might want to use the focus/exposure lock step without pressing the button all the way down for a lot of reasons:

- Focus lock takes a little time—a fraction of a second, but time nonetheless. If you're taking an action shot in which you want to precisely control the instant of exposure, lock the exposure and focus first; then wait with your finger on the shutter until you are absolutely ready to take the picture. Then, all it takes is a hair more pressure to capture the scene more or less instantly.

- If you want something that's off to the side of your picture to be in sharp focus—and this commonly is the case if you follow the rule of thirds—then point the camera at your off-center subject and lock the focus. Then recompose the shot to put the subject off to the side, and snap the picture.

Indeed, while some cameras are better than others, that pause is responsible for more frustration than all of the world's child-safe medicine bottles combined. Older digital cameras had a "shutter lag" that lasted a whole second or more, but even many of the newest digital cameras have some lag—and that's a real problem whether you're trying to freeze a NASCAR rounding the corner or catch your grandson hugging the dog.

Shutter lag happens because—invisible to you—digital cameras have a veritable checklist of tasks to perform when you press the shutter release. Not only does the camera need to measure the distance to the subject and lock in the proper focus, but it also has to measure the light, figure out how to balance the colors so whites look white and blue looks blue, calculate the best exposure, and lock in an aperture setting and shutter speed. The camera also has some obscure computer-like "housekeeping" chores to perform, like initializing the sensor chip and flushing buffers that hold data about your picture. You don't have to know what any of that means, just know that your camera is busy doing stuff as you start to take a picture.

If your camera's lag doesn't bother you, fine. You might have a camera with a short lag and, if that's the case, consider yourself lucky. But, if you want to minimize the lag, you can do a few things:

- The single biggest time-saver is using your camera's auto focus. If you prefocus your picture, you can save valuable milliseconds of lag.

- If you're more adventurous, you can also try presetting the camera's white balance based on the kind of scene you're shooting. If the white balance is set on auto, it'll have to adjust the colors in the image every time you take a picture, and that takes a little bit of time each time you press the shutter release. Instead, you can use the camera's menu to set the white balance for whatever lighting conditions you're shooting in, such as daylight, night, fluorescent, or incandescent lighting. Just remember to change the white balance for every new lighting situation you find yourself in.

- If you try those things and still find lag a problem, you may need to shoot *predictively*—and by that we mean to press the shutter release a heartbeat before you want to capture the photo. Measure the amount of lag your camera has—a half second? A second?—and start pressing the shutter release that far in advance.

- Some digital cameras try to get around the lag problem by offering a Continuous Fire or "Burst mode." When set to that position, you'll capture a series of pictures in quick succession, usually about 1/3 second apart. The presumption is that you'll get lucky and at least one of them will look good. Experiment with that mode and see if it helps you get better action shots.

Finally, you can try panning at the same time to better freeze your subject. See the section "Panning for Action" later in this chapter.

Stopping the Action

4

If your digital camera is an "all auto" point and shoot model, there's not a whole lot you can do to change your camera settings to help freeze the action—your camera is already programmed to try to use the fastest shutter speed it can most of the time. But you definitely can try your hand at panning, as we explain in the section "Panning for Action."

But, if your camera has a shutter priority setting—and many do—you're in luck: Shutter Priority mode was born for action photography. To freeze the action, you'll usually want to use the fastest shutter speed you can get your hands on— and Shutter Priority mode makes that easy to do. This is what Shutter Priority mode typically looks like—either an *A* or a Tv symbol:

In general, we recommend that you use the fastest shutter speed available to capture action. To do that, set your camera to Shutter Priority mode, and then use the controls on your camera to the fastest—or close to the fastest—shutter speed available. Good speeds for freezing action are 1/125, 1/1250, 1/500 second, or even faster. But if the shutter speed is really slow—like 1/60, 1/30, or, heaven forbid, 1/15 or slower, then it's pretty likely your picture will be blurry—but those shutter speeds are great for panning, which we'll talk about shortly.

What if your shutter speed just isn't fast enough to freeze the action? Bump up your camera's ISO, which we first talked about back in Chapter 3. Many cameras have an adjustable ISO level, which, like the film speed rating it's named after, lets you change the sensitivity of the camera to light. Increase the ISO level to enable you to shoot with a higher shutter speed.

Where the Controls Are

Of course, every camera's controls are a bit different, so we can't show you exactly how to operate yours. But many models are similar. Throughout the book, we use the Canon PowerShot A75, Olympus Stylus A410, and Sony CyberShot DSC-L1 as a guide to using your own camera.

Use Shutter Priority Mode or Action Mode

Switching out of Program or Auto mode can help you take better action shots.

On the *Canon PowerShot A75,* switch to Shutter Priority by turning the dial to Tv. To change the shutter speed, press the control dial on the back of the camera to the left or right. As you do so, you'll see the shutter speed change in the digital display on the back of the camera.

Or, you can try the Action mode—turn the dial to the running guy and start snapping pictures!

If you have a camera like the *Olympus Stylus A410* or the *Sony Cybershot DSC-L1*—which lacks an Action mode or Shutter Priority setting—then simply shoot in the default Program Auto mode.

4

Change the ISO

Want to make your camera more sensitive to light so you can take sharper pictures in low light? It helps to increase the ISO level.

On the Canon PowerShot A75, you need to be in Program, Aperture Priority, Shutter Priority, or Manual mode. You can't change ISO in Auto or any of the preset modes. Then press the FUNC button on the back of the camera and press the down arrow until ISO is selected on the digital display on the back of the camera. Finally, use the right arrow to increase the ISO to 100, 200, or 400, and press FUNC again to keep this setting.

The Olympus Stylus A410 doesn't let you set the ISO level, but the Sony CyberShot DSC-L1 does. On that camera, press the MENU button, and then nudge the control button to the left or right until you see the ISO menu. Move the control button up until you've selected 200 or 400, and then press MENU to save your changes.

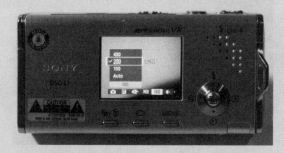

Continuous Fire

Another handy trick for taking action photos is to switch your camera to its Continuous Fire mode, which takes rapid fire photos as long as you hold down the shutter release.

On the Canon PowerShot A75, press the FUNC button on the back of the camera and press the down arrow until Drive mode, which looks like a square, is selected on the display on the back of the camera. Then press the right arrow on the control dial until the Continuous Fire mode (a bunch of squares lying on top of each other) is selected. Press the FUNC button again to save this setting. To get the fastest fire rate, turn off your flash. To do that, press the up arrow on the control dial until you see the flash icon with the slash through it.

To set the Olympus Stylus A410 to continuous fire, press the MENU/OK button, and then push the right arrow button to select the Mode menu on the digital display. Press the right arrow again and you'll see the ESP item selected. Use the down arrow until the Drive item is selected, and press the right arrow to enter the Drive menu. Finally, press the down arrow to select the Continuous Fire mode (it looks like a stack of squares). Press OK twice to save this setting. To get the fastest fire rate, turn off your flash. To do that, press the right arrow until you see the flash icon with a slash through it.

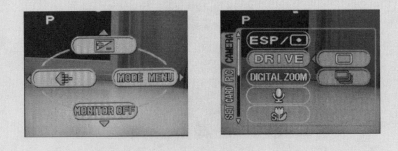

Panning for Action

Another really cool action photography technique called *panning* captures the subject in good, sharp focus, while "holding" the background as a motion blur. See

Figure 4-1 for an example of panning used to freeze a child's wild ride at a renaissance festival. This is a great technique to try for a couple of reasons:

- It gives the picture a great sense of motion. Freezing everything can make the picture look too static; panning lets you see that the subject is really ripping through the picture.

- It works well at slower shutter speeds. So, while your camera might usually blur an action shot in a bad way, panning lets you blur it in a good way.

Learning to pan takes a little practice. To create a good pan, you need to twist your body in sync with the motion of the subject as you press the shutter release. Here's how:

1. Position yourself where you can twist your body to follow the motion of the moving subject, without having the camera's line of sight blocked by something else.

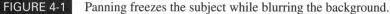

FIGURE 4-1   Panning freezes the subject while blurring the background.

2. If you can, set the camera's shutter speed for about 1/30. Feel free to experiment with this, but if you set the shutter speed too slow, you can't capture the subject effectively—it blurs. And, if the shutter is too fast, you won't get the contrasting blur in the background.

3. Twist your body with the motion of the subject and track it for a few seconds through the camera's viewfinder or on the LCD display. Keep the subject centered in the viewfinder, and then press the shutter release and continue tracking the subject for a few moments, even after you hear the picture get recorded. Just like in baseball or golf, ensure that you follow through the motion even after the shutter releases. That way, you don't stop panning in the middle of the exposure. You may need to practice this a few times to get the shot right, but your digital camera gives you the opportunity to practice 'til perfect, for free!

There's another way to show action—hold the camera rigidly in place and let the action scream through the viewfinder as you take the picture, capturing *its* motion, instead of the background's motion. If you're shooting in broad daylight with a reasonably fast shutter speed, you can hand-hold the camera for this kind of shot. If you're shooting with a slow shutter speed in a dark location, though, you might get better results mounting the camera on a tripod. Here's an example of capturing motion in a New York subway station at about 1/15 second:

Experiment with Action Mode

Your camera might have something called Action or Sports mode, like the one on the dial below (it looks like a running person).

If that's the case, consider using it to take these kinds of pictures. Action mode is usually designed to use the highest possible shutter speed available with no additional effort on your part. And that's great.

But, beware—not all Action modes work the same way. We've found that some cameras, when set to Action mode, disable focus locking. Most digital cameras lock in the focus the moment that you apply slight pressure to the shutter release, and we recommend using that technique to help reduce the inevitable shutter lag when taking pictures in fast-changing situations. With some model cameras, though, the lens will continue to autofocus, right up to the moment of exposure, even if you try applying some pressure to the shutter release. How does your camera work? You'll have to experiment with your camera to see. The easiest way is to put a little pressure on your shutter release button and move the camera around so it has to change focus from a nearby to a distant object. If the focus changes as you move, then give some thought to using Shutter Priority instead for hectic shooting, like at a soccer game.

Composing Action Shots

As in all kinds of photography, you can no doubt take some great pictures with your camera's zoom lens set on anything from its wide-angle position all the way up to the photographic equivalent of the Hubble telescope. And your camera's wide-angle setting can, in fact, have a role in action photography. But the essence of many action shots is a highly magnified immediacy—something you can only get with the lens zoomed all the way in to the telephoto position. Try zooming in tight for action shots—check out the difference between these pictures, and decide for yourself which one is more exciting:

Shooting Kids at Sporting Events

So, you're at a soccer game and trying to get some great pictures of your kid and the team. Here are a few pointers for getting great shots:

- Stay close to the action. If you can get close to or right on the sidelines, you won't have to shoot over or between other spectators. Getting closer also means that you don't have to zoom in all the way just to get something interesting in the frame—so your pictures won't be as shaky.

- Get down to their level. If you have little ones, get on your knees or on your belly, so you're taking pictures from their perspective. Often, they'll be a lot more interesting than photos that look down from five feet in the air, which is a towering height to a toddler.

- Keep the sun out of your eyes. If the sun is anywhere in your field of view, your pictures will be badly underexposed. Scout out a good spot before the game starts, so that you can keep the sun behind one of your shoulders. If you want to know the basics of exposure, check out Chapter 3.

- Whenever possible, try to frame the action as tightly as you can, meaning that only a few players are in the frame at once. If you're including the whole field in your shot, the scene will lack impact and it will be less interesting.

Shooting Animals

Animal photography—whether it's your family pet or a pack of wolves at the zoo—works best when you have a lot of zoom, a fast shutter speed, and a tripod. Try to fill the frame as much as possible, and expect the unexpected—like your subject suddenly darting out of your frame just when you get ready to snap the picture. Figure 4-2, for instance, shows a pair of wolves frolicking that would have been impossible to shoot without a fast shutter and a lens with a long reach.

Photographing Waterfalls

Have you ever seen those cool running-water shots in nature books and wished you could get the same sort of thing on your next vacation? Well, you can—it's easy to get images like this one:

Here's how:

■ You need to ensure that your camera will give you a long exposure, on the order of a half second. The best way to do this is to show up at the waterfall or running stream early in the morning or late in the afternoon, when there's not much light available.

 FIGURE 4-2   Wildlife photography requires many of the same shooting skills as action photography.

- Be sure that your camera's ISO setting is as low as it'll go, such as 100.

- Set your camera on a tripod (the long exposure absolutely requires a steady support—but you can use a very small, lightweight tripod).

- Compose the image and take the shot.

- If your camera allows it, take several pictures, each with a different shutter speed. The longer the shutter is open, the "smoother" the water will look.

Finally, you don't encounter waterfalls every day—so it pays to be prepared when you find one out in the real world. Practice at home! You can simulate a waterfall in your own kitchen. Check out the following pictures, shot in a kitchen sink. The first one was taken with the camera in Automatic mode. Then we set the camera to Shutter Priority and dialed the shutter speed to 1/30 second. Notice the picturesque way that the water rolls off our dirty dishes. Take a few of these sorts of images, and you'll be ready for a real waterfall!

Chapter 5

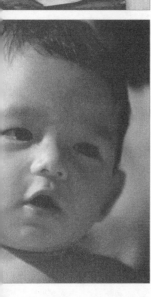

Viewing and Organizing Your Pictures

In this chapter you'll learn to...

- View pictures on your camera

- Erase pictures from your camera

- Understand the various kinds of memory cards

- Use a USB cable or card reader to copy images from the camera to the PC

- Care for memory cards

- Organize your images in Windows

- Transfer, rename, and categorize your images to reduce clutter

- Use organizer software to find your pictures more easily

- Archive your pictures on CD-ROM

- Install a new hard disk for additional storage

So far in this book, we've talked about how to take pictures. We covered the basics of composition, exposure, lighting, and so on. If you were shooting with a film camera, it might be time to pop out the film, drive to the supermarket, drop off your film, wait a few hours, pick up your film, and review the shots. You might discard the pictures you don't like and order reprints on those you do. Then you'd wait for the new pictures to arrive.

In digital, it's a lot easier. The pictures are stored on your camera's memory card, ready for inspection. In this chapter, we'll talk about working with those digital pictures—reviewing them on the camera, transferring them to your PC, organizing them, and getting the memory card ready for a new batch of pictures.

Viewing Pictures on Your Camera

One of the coolest things about digital photography is the ability to check your pictures on the spot. You can take a shot, instantly review it, and delete the image if you don't like it to make room for more photos. Or, you can see what's wrong—like red eye or a bad composition—and instantly reshoot the scene to try to do better. Let's start with what you can do on the camera, and then look at getting those pictures onto your computer.

Where the Controls Are

Of course, every camera's controls are a bit different, so we can't show you exactly how to operate yours. But many models are similar. Throughout the book, we use the Canon PowerShot A75, Olympus Stylus A410, and Sony CyberShot DSC-L1 as a guide to using your own camera. Let's review our pictures, transfer them to the PC, and, finally, delete the shots off the memory card with each of these cameras so you can see how it's done.

Canon PowerShot A75

The Canon PowerShot A75 has a review mode control on the back of the camera, right above the menu button. Slide it to the playback arrow, and use the right and left arrows on the control wheel to cycle through your pictures.

When you see a picture you want to get a closer look at, spin the zoom control on top of the camera toward its telephoto position. Every time you press the zoom, it magnifies the image by one step. You can then pan around the scene for a close look at the details using the four arrows on the control wheel. And here's a handy tip: if you are zoomed out all the way so you can see the tire image, zoom out one more notch to see thumbnail images of all the pictures on your camera. Then arrow over to the image and zoom in to see it in detail.

5

Don't like a picture? Then press the FUNC button to erase it—you'll have to press the set button in the control wheel to confirm the deletion.

When you're ready to transfer images to the computer, just plug it into the computer via its USB cable—the port is hidden behind the rubber A/V OUT cover on the side of the camera. Switch the camera on and set it to Playback mode. If you're using Windows XP, you won't even have to install any drivers; Windows should recognize the camera automatically.

When you're done transferring pictures to your computer, you can delete the copies that are still stored on the camera. To do that, be sure the camera is in Playback mode and press the menu button. You should see the Play menu.

Then arrow down to Erase All, arrow over to OK, and press the set button in the control wheel.

After a few moments, you'll be ready to take another batch.

Olympus Stylus A410

To switch to the A410's Playback mode, press the quick view button on the back of the camera. Now you can arrow to the left and right through your pictures.

> TIP *The up and down arrows will take you to the first and last pictures on the memory card.*

Like the Canon camera, the zoom control lets you magnify the current picture, and you can pan around inside the image using the four arrow buttons on the back of the camera. Zooming out past the picture's "full size" takes you to a thumbnail view of the pictures on the camera, which you can navigate using the left and right arrows.

If you want to delete a particular picture, press the OK button, and then press the down arrow to choose the Erase mode. You'll need to arrow to Yes, and then press OK again to delete the picture.

Want to copy pictures to your PC? Just plug in the camera's USB cable—its port is behind the memory card door—and press the OK button when you see PC selected in the USB menu in the digital display. Windows will automatically recognize the camera no matter which mode it is in.

After the pictures are copied to your PC and it's time to delete them from the camera, press Quick View, and then click the OK button. Press the right arrow to open the Mode menu, and then arrow down to the Card tab. Finally, press the right arrow twice to choose Card Setup, and then press OK to select Erase All. Of course, you'll have to arrow to Yes and press OK one more time to erase the images.

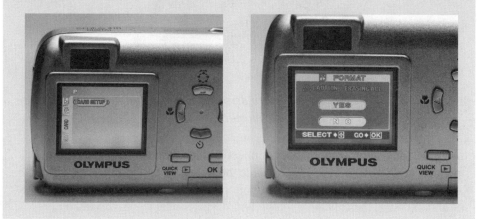

Sony CyberShot DSC-L1

The L1 works more or less the same as the other cameras in our inventory—it has a playback mode switch as well, this time on top of the camera to the left of the shutter release.

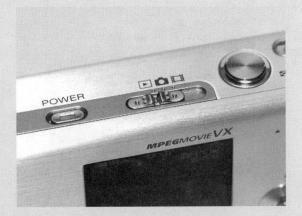

To view your pictures, slide the mode switch to the playback position on the left, and then arrow left and right through your images. Magnify the images with the zoom control, just as you would with either of the other models.

To delete a picture, press the Delete button (the leftmost button under the digital display), and then arrow up to Delete and push the joystick in to make the selection.

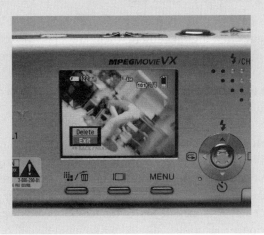

When you're ready to copy pictures to your PC, insert the USB cable into its port on the side of the camera—the port is hiding behind a little door right next to the lens. It doesn't matter which mode the camera is in. Windows will automatically recognize the camera as soon as you plug in the cable.

Finally, to delete the pictures on your Memory Stick, press the menu button and right arrow to the Setup mode. Arrow down to the Memory Stick Tool menu, and right arrow to the Format command. Click OK to erase the entire card.

The ABCs of Memory Cards

All digital cameras have to store their images somewhere. There's no single standard way of storing images in a digital camera; there are a half-dozen kinds of memory cards in use by cameras today, though it doesn't generally matter a lot which kind your camera uses. (Prices can vary, though—Memory Stick, for instance, is usually more expensive than Secure Digital or CompactFlash). Almost all cameras use one of these methods of storing images:

- **Internal memory** Although a few low-priced digital cameras use a few megabytes of internal, nonremovable memory for storing images, this is rare. More commonly, digital cameras include some internal memory—so you can take pictures even if no memory card is in your camera for some reason—but they also include one of the memory cards we mention elsewhere in this section.

■ **SmartMedia**   *SmartMedia* is the oldest of all memory formats and you won't find it in many new cameras, but if you own an older camera, it might contain this kind of card. It's paper thin and comes in capacities up to 128MB.

■ **CompactFlash**   While not as popular as Secure Digital (SD) cards these days—SD is smaller, and so it fits better into today's tiny cameras—CompactFlash is great because it's hands-down the cheapest kind of memory card you can buy. CompactFlash is reasonably small (it's about an eighth of an inch thick), yet it comes in capacities up to 4GB—as much storage space as a small hard disk. If you're looking to buy a high-megapixel camera or use your camera in situations where it's not easy to swap cards (such as underwater, if you're a scuba diver), then a CompactFlash-powered camera might be the right choice.

■ **Memory Stick**   You'll pretty much only find Memory Stick in Sony cameras, which makes these cards somewhat more expensive than other kinds of memory. Memory Stick also comes in an assortment of flavors: regular Memory Stick, Memory Stick Duo (a shorter version for small digital cameras), and Memory Stick Pro (which comes in gigabyte capacities— Memory Stick and Duo top out at 128MB). Each kind of Memory Stick only works in devices for which they were designed. A 4GB Memory Stick Pro card won't work in an older Memory Stick camera, for instance, and you can't put a Memory Stick in a Memory Stick Duo slot. Duo cards fit into adapters that make them work just like regular Memory Stick cards, though. Bottom line: buy Memory Stick media carefully because there are so many similar (but incompatible) variations.

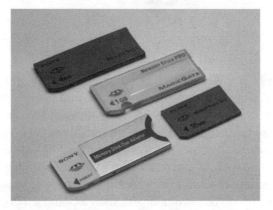

■ **Secure Digital (SD)**   More commonly referred to by the abbreviation SD, Secure Digital has become the most popular memory card around, filling the slots of a majority of popular cameras.

■   **xD**   It has a wacky name, but xD is the newest kind of memory card and is found in cameras from a few companies, but mostly Olympus. Like Sony's Memory Stick, xD cards cost a bit more than SD or CompactFlash.

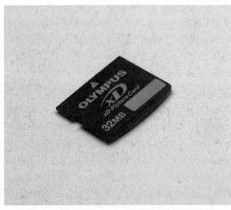

■   **Floppy disk and CD-R**   Many older Sony digital cameras used a floppy disk to store pictures. The advantage: floppy disks were ubiquitous. There were no confusing image transfer procedures, because you just pull the floppy out of the camera and insert it into the PC's floppy disk drive. On the other hand, floppy disks only hold 1.44MB of data—a tiny amount compared to any other memory card format. Floppy disks are also fairly slow. Those disadvantages add up to cameras that simply couldn't take high-resolution images, and they suffered from a long lag between when the image was taken and when it was written to memory. These cameras are largely relegated to the dustbin of history, but Sony now sells cameras that write pictures to a recordable CD disc. These cameras suffer from all the same limitations as the floppy disk models. Our advice? Avoid them.

Transferring Images to Your PC

No matter what kind of digital camera or removable media you use, eventually you'll want to get your pictures from the camera to a computer. Think of your computer as a photographic base of operations: it's from there that you'll be able to edit, print, and share your pictures. Your digital camera comes with software for transferring images and a cable that you can use to connect the camera to your PC.

Memory Card Glitches

We sometimes hear about memory cards that seem to "die." If your memory card has stopped working, what's the problem?

First, remember that memory cards are pretty delicate. If you've damaged the card, which isn't altogether out of the question, it's now a really, really small coaster. Throw it away with the knowledge that you can replace it for just a few dollars.

An engineer from a leading memory card company has told us that there are other possibilities as well. It seems that using the same memory card in multiple devices can change the formatting or fill certain areas of the card with gibberish, rendering it unable to store digital pictures. So don't use the same SmartMedia card in your MP3 player and digital camera. If you're having trouble with your card, try to revive the card by using the Format command in your camera's menu system. But if that doesn't work, you're probably out of luck.

Nearly all digital cameras come with a USB cable to connect the camera to the computer. If you have an old camera, it might have a serial cable (you can tell it's a serial cable if one end has nine pins sticking out). Serial cables are hard to use: they require special software, are prone to unexpected glitches, and you shouldn't plug them in when the computer is powered on. If you have such a beast, consider upgrading to a newer computer that uses USB.

USB cables are smarter, faster, and rarely experience unexpected connection problems. You can even plug and unplug them with the computer turned on. You can see both ends of a typical digital camera USB cable in the following illustration. The end on the right plugs into the computer in any narrow rectangular USB port; the end on the left plugs into the camera.

How to ...   Connect Your Camera with USB

If you have a USB-enabled camera and PC, the transfer process is easy. Here's a general overview of how to do it:

1. Start by installing the software that came with your camera. If you have a fairly new camera—one made in the last three years—then you probably don't even have to do this step unless Windows refuses to recognize your camera in Step 4. Windows automatically works with most digital cameras without the need to install any additional software.

2. Connect the USB cable to your computer's USB port and to the camera. You don't have to turn off your computer to do this, even if you have to disconnect an existing USB device to free up a port.

3. Turn on the camera. If the transfer doesn't automatically work, you may need to check your camera's user guide to see if it has a special "transfer" or "PC" mode. Connect the camera to AC power if you can.

4. The computer should automatically recognize the camera and start the transfer software. Now you can copy the images from the camera to a folder on the computer.

Transfer Shortcuts: Using Memory Card Readers

Just because your camera comes with a serial or USB cable, that doesn't mean you have to use it. Memory adapters (also called card readers), which are gadgets that let you insert a memory card and read images from it like a floppy disk, let you easily transfer images to the computer without repeatedly messing with cables. There are several advantages to using card readers:

■ You can conserve camera battery power because the camera isn't used in the transfer.

■ You don't have to frequently get to the back of your computer to connect or disconnect cables.

■ Transfers may be faster with a card reader.

■ You can avoid confusing transfer software because card readers let you drag-and-drop images directly to a folder on your hard disk.

Using a Card Reader

The kind of card reader you choose depends largely upon the kind of removable memory that your camera uses. Most attach to your computer via USB cable.

■ **Desktop single format card readers**   For $15 or $20, you can get a card reader that accepts the specific kind of memory card your digital camera uses. There are readers for CompactFlash, SmartMedia, SD, and Memory Stick, and even xD. The downside? If you ever need to read a different kind of memory card—like from a second camera or a digital music player— you'll need to buy a second card reader, which will eat up a second USB port and more desk space.

■ **Desktop all-in-one readers**   Just like cameras that are starting to accommodate more than one kind of memory card, readers are becoming more flexible as well. For $30 or $40, you can get a universal card reader, which can accommodate six or more kinds of memory cards, making it easy to read and write to cards for your digital camera, MP3 player, and PDA all from the same device.

Memory Card: Fact and Fiction

Let's dispel some myths about memory cards.

Removable memory cards are nothing more than digital storage for your camera, which means that memory cards aren't designed to store images of a certain size. Some people mistakenly believe that if they want to store images of a larger or smaller pixel size, they need a different memory card. Memory cards are completely standardized and interchangeable, and they don't particularly care what you store on them. In fact, you don't even have to put digital images on them at all. Memory cards will hold sound files, text documents—anything that you can put on your hard drive. Your camera won't know what to do with files like that and will consequently ignore such files, but you can store anything on a memory card.

There are differences between memory cards, though. The principal difference is speed—cards are rated at speeds like 2x, 4x, and 8x. The faster ones write data faster and are a good choice if you value speed when taking pictures. They're also good for high-megapixel cameras because large files take longer to record. On the other hand, faster cards tend to cost more.

■ **Internal card readers**   For the ultimate in convenience, you can find card readers that fit in one of your PC's empty drive bays. Y-E Data (www.yedata .com), for instance, sells the excellent 7-in-1 reader that packs six kinds of memory card slots into a floppy disk drive. Replace your existing floppy disk drive and have access to any memory card (except xD) right from your PC.

Caring for Your Memory Cards

After you are done transferring images from the memory card to your PC, you no longer need those images. You can delete them to make room for more pictures. There are two ways to do this: you can delete them via the PC, or use the camera's controls to delete images from the card. If your memory card is inserted in the PC via some sort of memory card adapter, using the PC doesn't waste camera battery power, and that's a good reason to do it that way. If you don't have that luxury, a good idea is to plug the camera into its AC adapter so you don't drain your camera's batteries.

To delete images from your memory card via the PC, you can usually just select the files and press the DELETE key on your keyboard; it's just like deleting any kind of file from your PC's floppy or hard disk.

To delete images using the camera's interface, you'll have to navigate the camera's menu system. Typically, you'll have the option of deleting a single image or all the images on the disk at once. Be careful—this operation cannot be undone.

In addition to deleting images from your memory cards, you should take other precautions to ensure that your cards live a long and fruitful life. After all, memory cards can be expensive. Keep the following tips in mind:

- Avoid leaving memory cards in direct sunlight for a long time.

- Don't put memory cards in your back pocket or other places where they can get bent, broken, or crushed. That's particularly true for SmartMedia cards and floppy disks, which can break with modest amounts of force.

- Keep your cards empty whenever possible. All memory cards look alike, and the last thing you need is to put a memory card in your camera while on vacation only to discover it's still full of images that you never saved to your PC from last time. Transfer images to the PC promptly, and then erase the card.

- Never write directly on the surface of your memory cards or put stickers on them to track their contents. That can damage the card or the camera.

Recovering Lost Pictures

Have you ever accidentally deleted an important file, noticing it was gone an instant after you sent it irretrievably to the trash? All you can really do is shout, "d'oh!"

The same thing can happen to pictures on a memory card. Thankfully, when you erase a card, the files aren't necessarily gone right away—the memory card simply "forgets" it is holding data. If you need to get back lost images, you might consider a program like ImageRecall, from www.flashfixers.com. This simple program recovers deleted images, movies, and other data from removable memory cards. It works with any removable media, from SmartMedia and Compact Flash to Memory Stick and SD Cards.

ImageRecall scans the contents of a card, restoring lost files to a folder on your PC's hard disk as it goes. Just remember that if you plan to run ImageRecall on a memory card, do it before you use the card for anything else. Adding new data to your card can damage "deleted" pictures already on the card, lowering the odds that you'll get anything useful from the recovery process.

What are the odds you'll ever need this program? Pretty low, probably. But if you do find yourself with a dead memory card or lost pictures, ImageRecall might be worth a try.

Managing Your Digital Pictures

5

Once your pictures are on your computer, they can become tricky to find. After all, it doesn't take long to rack up hundreds or even thousands of pictures—and then finding a specific one can be like finding a needle in a haystack.

We recommend that you store your images in a single folder or set of folders, instead of spreading them all over your hard disk. Most versions of Windows have a folder called *My Pictures* for storing images, and we suggest you use it.

TIP | *If you are using Windows Me or Windows XP, you'll find the My Pictures folder inside the My Documents folder.*

You can store your images anywhere, but My Pictures is a great place. It's easy to remember, and many photo applications will automatically look here for pictures.

Now that you have a main folder for storing your images, you might want to create *subfolders,* which are folders inside your main folder (like My Pictures) that let you organize your pictures more precisely. As you can see in Figure 5-1, you can sort your pictures into a myriad of folders that help you find specific images by category, event, purpose, date, or genre.

Renaming Images

Now that you have an organizational system for arranging your images, it's time to think about filenames.

It's often a good idea to immediately rename your images and categorize them into specific folders when you first import them onto your PC. What happens if you put this off till later? You might end up with a few batches of 50 images each that need to be renamed. The task will eventually get too daunting, and you'll have untold pictures with obscure filenames that need to be renamed.

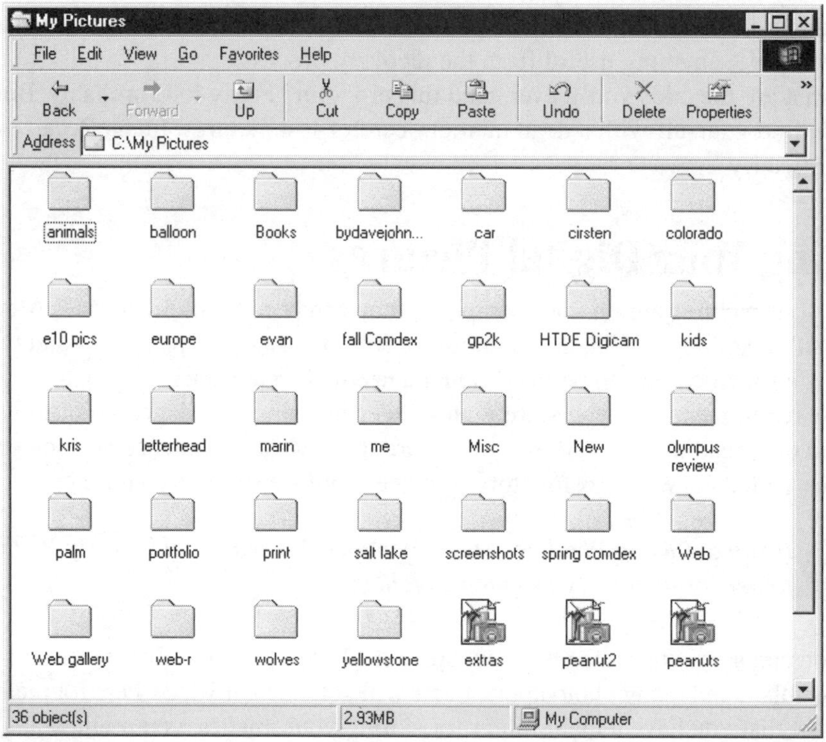

FIGURE 5-1 The more subfolders you use, the easier it should be to find the right image in a pinch.

Here's an easy strategy for renaming your images:

1. Open the folder in which your newly transferred images are stored.

2. If you are using Windows Me or Windows XP, you should be able to see a preview of the image in the folder. If you can't, choose View | Filmstrip or View | Thumbnails from the folder's menu. Look at the first photo and decide what you want to name it.

3. Right-click on the photo and choose Rename from the menu. Type the name of the file and press the ENTER key.

4. Repeat the process with the other images in the folder.

5. When you are done, you can drag images into appropriate subfolders in the My Pictures folder and delete the empty temporary folder.

If you want a better view of a picture in the folder, you can always just double-click it. Windows will display it in the Windows Picture and Fax Viewer. You can use the scroll wheel on your mouse to zoom in and out when you're in the viewer.

Faster Renaming

Ideally, you'll rename all of your photos as you transfer them to your PC—that way, it's a bit easier to find them whenever you need a specific image. But let's be honest, sometimes that's just too much work. If you simply want to change the name of your files from totally indecipherable, like P7281775, to something that reflects the overall theme of the batch, like Summer Vacation, then you can do that as well.

Select all of the photos in the folder. You can do that by choosing Edit | Select All from the folder's menu, or you can click the first picture in the folder, scroll to the last image, and click again, holding down the SHIFT button on your keyboard.

Shift Selecting, as it's called, lets you choose all the files between the first and last click in a single action.

> **TIP** *Only want to select a few images? Press the CTRL key on your keyboard as you click the mouse to choose only certain images.*

Right-click on one of the selected images—it doesn't matter which one—and choose Rename from the menu. Type a new name and press the ENTER key. Your pictures will all be given the new name, with a number in parentheses so you can tell them apart.

Browsing for Pictures

Even with a slew of subfolders, finding specific images on your hard disk can be difficult if you just root through folders in Windows. Even with descriptive filenames and lots of aptly titled subfolders, it can be a challenge to locate "that picture of Tim playing with the puppies" you took two years ago. Forget the needle in a haystack; it's akin to finding a needle within a stack of other needles.

Filenames and folders are great, but there's no substitute for seeing your images—browsing for pictures, as it were. That's why the best way to look for pictures is often with a software program designed just for that purpose.

Using a Photo Organizer

Photo organizers help you zero in on the right picture by browsing for it visually. You can choose from quite a number of organizers. Here are our favorites:

- Shutterfly (www.shutterfly.com)
- Adobe Photoshop Elements (www.adobe.com)
- Picasa (www.picasa.com)
- Microsoft Digital Image Suite (www.microsoft.com)
- ACDSee (www.acdsee.com)

Using any of these offerings, you can typically search for images visually, by keyword, by date, or by filename. Shutterfly's Free Text Search, for instance, lets you find pictures based on the text you enter. This search looks for the text you entered in all picture titles and messages intended to print on the backs of pictures.

To conduct a Free Text Search in Shutterfly, click the green View & Enhance button on the main navigation bar. With Shutterfly, you can find pictures based on the text associated with a picture. This search looks for the text entered in all picture titles and descriptions as well as messages intended for printing on the backs of photos. You can also search according to time period. For visual searches, Shutterfly's small picture view lets you see many images at once so you can find your photo quickly, while its large thumbnail view lets you see the image details for each photo. You can choose which viewing option best suits your needs. Additionally, Shutterfly lets you mark your best photos as "favorites" so you can find them easily to create a special slide show or end-of-year project, such as a photo calendar.

Picasa and Adobe Photoshop Elements help you search according to time period. Picasa has a great Timeline mode that lets you navigate through a carousel of pictures. When you find a stack of pictures you want from a particular time period, click to launch a slide show. Adobe Photoshop Elements has a timeline across the top of the screen that helps you zero in on a desired time period, and its "tags" let you assign keywords to your pictures, and then search for those keywords later just by clicking on the word in the tag pane.

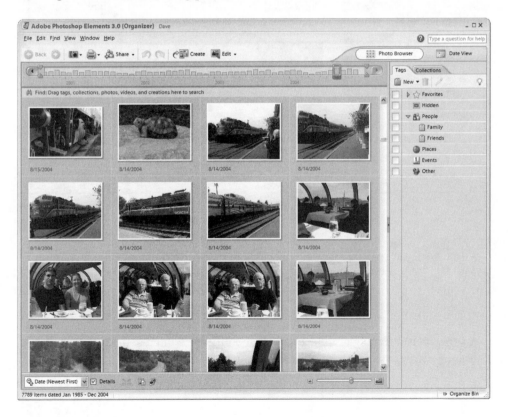

Microsoft's Digital Image Suite has a Library program that works much the same way. It has a floating Keyword Painter palette that you can use to dab keywords onto pictures with your mouse, which makes it a snap to find all the pictures of a grandson or cousin, no matter where they are on your computer or when you took them.

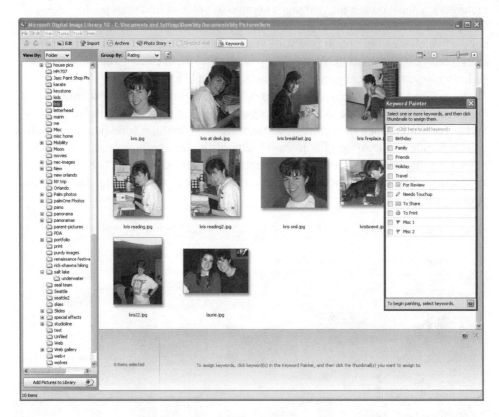

How to Use Keywords

A *keyword* is a term that you can use to identify the contents, theme, or style of an image. Suppose you have this witty picture, for instance:

You might want to associate the following keywords with this image: **kids**, **puppy**, **Evan**, **Trance**. When you search for all your pictures that have the word "kids" or "Evan" in their description, this image should appear in the list. Keywords are a pretty "manual" operation, though. You need to decide what keywords to use and enter them all by hand in whatever organizer you use that supports this feature. If your cataloging software supports keywords, though, a little effort up front can make it quite easy to find that proverbial needle in the haystack.

Archiving Images

Eventually, your collection of digital images may grow too large for your PC's hard disk. If that's the case, you have a few choices:

- Delete some images from your hard disk.

- Archive the images someplace, like on CD or DVD.

- Add another hard disk for additional storage space.

Deleting images is the easiest route, but it is the most painful. No one ever wants to delete pictures. If you're like us, you probably want to save most of your images forever. Instead, consider archiving your images.

Shutterfly offers you the ability to store the photos you've uploaded to Shutterfly on an Archive CD, which starts at $9.99. You simply select the photo albums you want to save onto the CD, and Shutterfly does the work for you. The company will put all the original high-resolution versions of the images, just as you uploaded them, on a nonerasable Mac and PC-compatible CD. Shutterfly will even label your CD with a name and date for easy reference. In a few days, you'll have your CD that you can store in a safe place.

If you have a CD-RW or DVD recorder, you can do this yourself. You can copy hundreds of images to a disc (depending upon the file size) that will last more or less forever. CDs do degrade over time, but they will last for decades. To be sure your images are protected, you can make a new copy of your CD or DVD every 10 or 20 years—or, more realistically, copy the images to whatever technology is popular then, like nuclear bionic laser holographic kneepads. Or whatever.

A CD-RW drive is a kind of CD drive that can write to blank discs, while DVD writers come in several varieties, the most common of which is DVD-R/RW and DVD+R/W. Most of these drives come with software like Adaptec's Easy CD and DVD Creator (www.adaptec.com), seen in Figure 5-2, or perhaps Nero

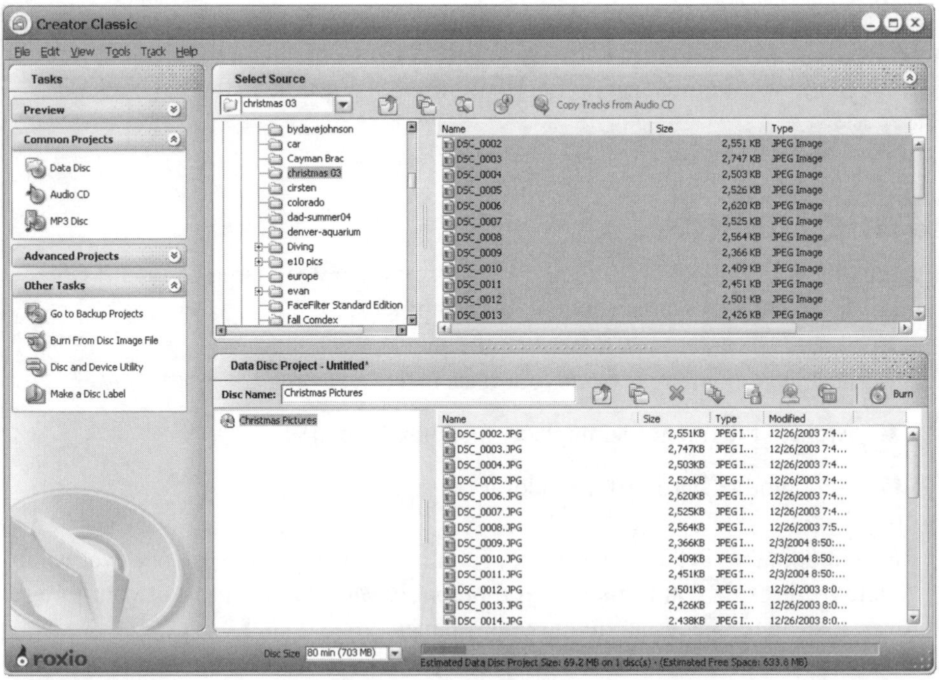

FIGURE 5-2   CD burning software makes it easy to copy blank images to a CD.

(www.nero.com). These programs let you simply drag-and-drop image files from the hard disk to the CD, and then "burn" the disc, a process that takes a few minutes to copy all the data to the CD. After it's done, the CD-R is playable in any computer with a CD-ROM drive.

If you have Windows XP and a CD-RW drive, you don't even need any additional software: just open a folder with images and select the images you want to copy to the CD. Then click Copy to CD from the Picture Tasks pane on the left side of the folder. After a few moments, you'll see a balloon in the System Tray that says **You have files waiting to be written to the CD**. Place a blank CD in your drive and open My Computer. Right-click on the blank CD and choose **Write these files to CD**. It's a bit more complicated than using a program like Roxio or Nero, but it's free.

Adding an Extra Hard Drive

One other option you might consider is adding another hard disk. Hard drives get cheaper and bigger every year, and these days 200GB drives are neither unusual nor are they particularly expensive. Some people install a second drive and dedicate it for images, video, music, and other multimedia files.

If you don't want to mess around inside your PC, you can add an external hard disk instead. These days, USB 2.0 and FireWire (also known as i.Link or IEEE1394) hard disks are fast, inexpensive, and install in just minutes by doing nothing more than plugging in a cable. We highly recommend these sorts of external drives.

5

Chapter 6

Quick Changes for Your Images

In this chapter you'll learn to...

■ Determine system requirements for editing images on a PC

■ Choose an image processing program

■ Open and edit images

■ Change the resolution of digital images for e-mail, the Web, and other applications

■ Save an image in a different file format

■ Crop images to improve composition

■ Rotate images taken with the camera on its side

■ Fix a crooked image

■ Change color to black and white

■ Change the brightness in an image

■ Correct the color balance in a picture

One of the most exciting advantages of using a digital camera is the flexibility and control it gives you for tweaking and improving your images. Don't like your composition? Change it. You can crop your pictures just a little to subtly improve their appearance, or radically change the look of a picture by turning its orientation from landscape to portrait. You can fix a crooked horizon, resize an image for e-mail, tweak the colors or brightness of an image—it's all up to you.

These are things that until recently were difficult or impossible to do without a darkroom. These days, you can experiment endlessly. It never costs you a penny until you're ready to print the final result, because it's all done with pixels on a computer screen. As long as you're careful not to save over the original file, you can make as many different versions as you like.

In this chapter, we'll get started with image editing. This is the place to turn to for the most common kinds of corrections—simple things you can do to your images without learning a whole lot about the art and science of image editing.

How Much PC You Need

You're probably expecting us to tell you that you should have the fastest PC you can afford—like a 10 GHz Pentium 5, perhaps. And aside from the fact that computers haven't gotten that fast yet, you don't really need quite that much speed. To be perfectly honest, you probably *should* work with the fastest PC that you can afford. Image editing, especially if you really get into it and work with lots of three- or five-megapixel images, is a horsepower-intensive task. The more computer that you've got pushing pixels around, the more fun you'll have. A slow PC can sometimes be frustrating, because it'll take longer to work and might even take a while to redraw the screen.

Here's what we think you should have, as a minimum, to do image editing without getting an ulcer:

6

- **Pentium III processor**   We used to do image editing on a 200MHz Pentium (now known as a Pentium Classic) running Windows 3.1, so it can obviously be done with pretty much any computer. But it's slow. A much better configuration: try to get at least a 1-GHz processor to push all those pixels around. Right-click on My Computer to read about your PC's processor on the General tab.

- **256MB of RAM**   Here's where spending just a little extra can really pay off. If your PC has at least 512MB of RAM, image editing will seem much faster, even with a slower processor. That's because high-megapixel images occupy lots of room in memory, and if they can't fit there, Windows stores parts of them on the hard disk. That can make something as simple as a screen redraw drag on forever. Is there value in having a gigabyte of memory? There sure is—if you have several large images open at once, your system won't slow down as it would with less memory. Many new PCs are now shipping with 1GB of memory (that's 1000MB), so 512MB certainly isn't an unusual amount of memory. Right-click on My Computer and check the General tab to see how much memory your PC has installed.

- **60GB hard drive**   This might be the single most important part of a computer that works with lots of digital photos. Hard drives are really cheap now, so you should have lots of room to store your images. The bigger the better, but unless you also want to make digital video, you probably don't need a super-monstrous hard disk. A second hard disk or a CD-RW drive for archiving old images can come in handy as well. To see how big your computer's hard disk is, you can double-click My Computer, and then click the icon for the hard disk. Look at the Details on the left side of the folder to see what your drive's size is.

Choosing an Image Editor

Before you can get started editing images, you might want to invest in an editing program. Any one will do, at least at first. For the most part, all image editors give you the ability to do certain things, such as:

- Resize your images

- Apply paint to your image, using a set of brushes and other paint tools

- Add text and other graphics

- Crop pictures and make selections within your picture

- Combine multiple images into a new composition

- Use controls to change aspects of your image, like the color, sharpness, or brightness and contrast

So which image editing program is for you? Well, you might want to start with a free one. If your digital camera came with an image editor of some sort, you might want to give it a spin and see if you like the way it works.

Ultimately, though, you may opt to invest in a more sophisticated program. These programs tend to have both automatic and manual editing tools.

Automatic tools are usually wizards, which are step-by-step procedures that lead you easily through a task to change the image for you, more or less automatically. They adjust the colors and brightness in an image, remove red eye in flash photography, and perform a host of other minor miracles without much real input from you. The downside, of course, is that the final result is not always what you expect. Feel free to try the automatic stuff, but remember that you can use the Undo button to revert to the original image anytime you don't like the results.

Most image editors also include lots of manual doohickeys that give you more control and power, but of course you have to master the interface before you can see improvements in your images. Perhaps the most famous image editor of all time is Adobe PhotoShop, seen in Figure 6-1. The downside is that the program has a somewhat steep learning curve. Another alternative is PhotoShop Elements. I really like the way Adobe has combined the best parts of PhotoShop with a simpler interface that's designed for ordinary folks, not graphics professionals. Elements is a wonderful program.

Another alternative is Paint Shop Pro from Jasc (www.jasc.com). This image editing program has about 75 percent of the features found in PhotoShop, but at a fraction of the cost and with a much simpler interface. Throughout the rest of this

Do It in Shutterfly: Image Editing

Keep in mind that you don't have to have an image editor on your computer
at all. Shutterfly has its own image editing tools, which you can use for free.
Check out the four editing tabs to the right of your picture in Shutterfly, which
let you remove red eye, crop, add special effects, and enhance your picture with
attractive captions and borders (see the following illustration).

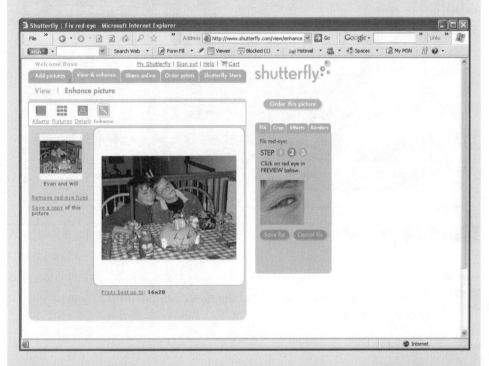

You can use Shutterfly to make important changes to your photos. We think
that's great. If you want to make some prints in Shutterfly, you can crop the
photos, add captions, and do other tweaks without ever opening a big image
editor. In this book, we'll show you how to do this stuff both ways—with an
image editor and with Shutterfly. Look for the **Do It in Shutterfly** boxes for
details throughout the rest of the book.

book we'll generally use Paint Shop Pro to illustrate techniques. Keep in mind, though,
that you can use any software you like, but the actual mouse and keystrokes will
differ somewhat depending upon what program you choose to use.

FIGURE 6-1   PhotoShop is an outstanding program, but all of its features can be intimidating.

You can download a trial version of Paint Shop Pro from the Jasc web site at www.jasc.com, and a trial version of Photoshop Elements from www.adobe.com.

How to ...   Open an Image in Paint Shop Pro

Because we're going to spend some time in Paint Shop Pro over the next few chapters, let's take a quick look at how to use the program. Start Paint Shop Pro by choosing it from the Windows Start menu. There are three ways to open an image in Paint Shop Pro—you can use whichever method you find easiest.

■   Choose File | Open from the main menu and navigate your way to the image you want to open in the Open dialog box. Double-click on the file, or select it and click the Open button.

■ Choose File | Browse from the main menu. The Browse window appears, which shows a set of thumbnails in the right pane and a directory tree of your hard disk on the left. An example follows. When you select a hard disk folder, its contents appear on the right. Just double-click an image to open it. The Browse window remains open in case you want to open more images in this way.

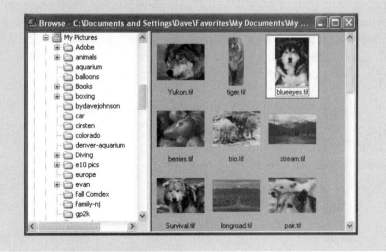

■ Open the folder with the image you want to open directly on the Windows desktop, and drag the image file from the folder to the Paint Shop Pro window. If Paint Shop Pro isn't on top, you can do this instead: drag the image file out of the folder and hold it over the Paint Shop Pro button in the task bar at the bottom of the Windows desktop. Don't let go of the file yet; just hold it there for a few moments. Paint Shop Pro should pop to the front. Finally, move the file up to the Paint Shop Pro window and let go.

Changing the Picture File

Some of the time, you'll only need to make minor changes to your images. In the next few sections, we'll show you how to make changes to the file itself, like resizing the picture and changing the file format of your digital images.

Shrinking Your Images

As Jebediah Springfield, founder of the animated city in *The Simpsons,* once said, "A noble spirit enbiggens the smallest man." If *The Simpsons* can make up a word, so can we—so this section is all about de-biggening your pictures.

Why would you want to do that? Well, 3- and 5-megapixel images are great, but they're just too big for some situations. Suppose you want to e-mail some pics to friends and family, for instance. A 3.3-megapixel image, which measures about 2048×1536 pixels, is just too big for that—such a big picture would clog up the recipient's e-mail account. What you might want to do instead is to de-biggen your images.

How small is small enough? If all you want to do is share a picture for e-mail, you probably want to shrink the file so that its longest dimension—either length or width, depending upon the orientation of the image—is no more than about 600 pixels. Here's how to do it in Paint Shop Pro:

1. Open Paint Shop Pro and load the file that you want to resize.

2. Choose Image | Resize.

3. Because we want to make the image a specific pixel size, make sure Pixels is selected on the right side of the dialog box. We could also change the size of the image based on percentage or print size, but we don't need those options now.

4. Make sure the dialog box is set to resize all layers and to maintain the aspect ratio of the image (you can find these options at the bottom of the dialog box). Also set Resample Using to Smart Size. This tells Paint Shop Pro to use the highest quality method for resizing the image to generate the best final result.

5. Finally, enter the new dimensions for your image. You only need to enter the height or the width, and because the aspect ratio isn't changing, Paint Shop Pro will fill in the other number for you automatically. In the following image, for instance, we entered **600** for the height and Paint Shop Pro automatically set the width to 501 pixels to keep the picture's proportions correct.

6. Click OK to resize the image.

7. You should see the image shrink on the screen. You can now click Save—destroying the original—or save it as a new file so you retain the original's larger pixel size. To save it as the old filename, choose File | Save from the main menu. Otherwise, choose File | Save As and give the image a new name.

 You may have noticed that you can make images bigger using this procedure as well. You shouldn't do that, though, because you'll just end up with a blurry enlargement.

photo collages

▶ **Make a collage** of your favorite photos and send them to friends and family.

► **This is a challenging scene**. If you expose details in the dark jacket, the sunbeams in the background will be overexposed. If you expose the background perfectly, the jacket will be a dark blob. Your best bet—use the camera's automatic exposure meter and focus on her face.

removing objects

> **Sometimes tourists** can get in the way of a beautiful scene. Using a "clone" tool, you can erase them from your picture!

photo books

Michael's First Masterpiece

▶ **Last summer** when Shutterfly customer Anne M.'s basement flooded in Columbus, OH, her children's art projects were ruined. "Now I scan my kids' projects into the computer and combine them with pictures of the artist. At the end of the year I make a photo book to commemorate these treasures."

spiral-bound photo albums

Where We Got Engaged!

▶ **Shutterfly** customer Jeff D. of Leominster, MA, proposed to his fiancée in Paris, France. "I created a Snapbook album that traced our relationship from the day we met...The last page contained a photo of me holding a single rose with the caption 'And then...' At that point, I pulled out the ring and asked her to marry me."

▶ **Louis V. of Valley Stream, NY,** turned a Father's Day photo of his grandchildren and himself into a t-shirt. "I added the caption, 'We love you Poppy' and made the t-shirt using Shutterfly... I love it!"

▶ **Shutterfly user Susie K**. lives in San Francisco and her parents live in Atlanta, so they don't get to see each other as often as they'd like. "To keep in touch and help my parents feel more connected to their grandbaby, I snap and send them pictures of our son's special moments. And at the end of the year I give my parents a calendar of their favorite snapshots."

▶ **Every holiday season** Courtney N. of Barrington, IL, sends a photo greeting card to her friends and family. "After I designed my cards, I uploaded my address book and used Shutterfly to print, seal, stamp, and mail them for me."

NOTE   *Most image editors have very similar features. If you want to resize an image in Photoshop Elements, for instance, choose Image | Resize | Image Resize from the menu and enter your changes in the Pixel Dimensions section atop the dialog box.*

Saving Images in Different File Formats

Sometimes you may want to change the file format of a picture, such as from JPG to TIF. Why? Two main reasons:

■ Sometimes the program you're using or the recipient of your picture can't handle the file format the picture is originally stored in. If you have a bunch of photos stored in TIF format, for instance, and want to turn them into a slide show using some cool new photo slide show program you just got, you might be surprised to learn that the program can't read TIF. You'll need to convert the pictures to JPGs first.

■ Another reason is to preserve image quality. Every time you edit, and then resave an image in JPG format, it loses a little quality. Generally, this isn't a big deal, but if you are editing an important photograph and plan to print it at a really large size, you want to preserve as much image quality as possible during the editing process. Saving a file as a TIF (as they say in the sandwich bag industry) locks in the image quality. You can convert it back to a JPG at the end, right before you upload it to Shutterfly for printing.

Right about now, you might be feeling aghast that the JPG format "leaks" image quality. And you might be thinking, "Why not just set the camera to take pictures in TIF format right from the start?"

That's a good question. Many digital cameras can take pictures in the TIF format. But that's not a good solution. The TIF format makes really big picture files, and it can take a long time (as much as a minute per shot) to save those pictures to your memory card. So TIF is a clumsy format for taking pictures. And let's be perfectly honest: there will be snooty digital photographers who adopt a fake English accent and claim that they only shoot in TIF format to preserve all the image quality; the reality is that you don't lose much by using JPG. We only recommend using TIF in rare situations where small differences in image quality might really be visible—such as editing a picture and then printing it at poster size—and that's not often.

NOTE *Just looking at a JPG file doesn't affect the image quality. So you can open it in an image editor or picture viewer, look at it, and close it again without reducing the quality.*

So here's how to change a picture's file format:

1. Open the image in Paint Shop Pro.

2. Choose File | Save As from the main menu.

3. In the Save As Type drop-down menu, choose the file format you need.

4. If necessary, click the Options button to fine-tune the file format. The Options button lets you specify the amount of image compression, number of colors the image will be saved in, and other properties. When you're saving a JPG picture, you can always adjust the amount of compression that's used. This sets the file size—the bigger the file, the higher the quality, and the smaller the file, the lower the visual quality. We always save our JPGs with the slider very close to the highest quality end of the spectrum. You can always shrink it later.

5. Click OK to save the file.

After saving the file, you'll have two copies—one called **my_picture.jpg** and one called **my_picture.tif**. You can delete the older file, or if you might still need it, keep both copies. Of course, when you look at two files with the same name but different file extensions on the Windows desktop, it can be hard to tell them apart. If in doubt, right-click on the file and choose Properties from the menu. Verify the type of file before you possibly delete the wrong file.

Do It in Shutterfly: Photo Enhancements

When you choose to make prints in Shutterfly, the site automatically analyzes your pictures and applies adjustments to improve the exposure and colors for better looking prints. This process is called VividPics, so if you see the term on the site, know that it's referring to a set of automatic improvements that happens before printing.

Can you turn off VividPics? Absolutely. If you'd rather not have these automatic changes happen to your pictures, click the View & Enhance tab, and then click Effects. On the left, check Don't Apply Automatic Corrections to Picture.

One Step Photo Enhancement

As we said earlier, even advanced image editors with lots of manual controls usually give you easy, one-step tools for improving your images. Our advice: definitely try the quick-fix approach just to see if it helps the image. If it does, great! Save the image and get on with your day. If you don't like the results, the Undo button is just one mouse click away.

What are we talking about? Check out Paint Shop Pro, which has an Enhance Photo button in the Photo toolbar atop the screen. Click it and select One Step Photo Fix to make Paint Shop Pro run a slew of corrections on your picture, including color balance, contrast, and sharpness. You can also run these corrections one at a time by choosing them from the menu under Enhance Photo. Either way, they let you optimize a picture quickly with little to no effort on your part.

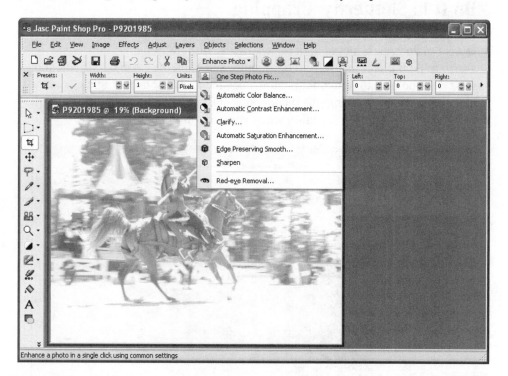

6

TIP *If you have Adobe Photoshop Elements, you can take advantage of a few Auto levels in the Enhance menu.*

Improving Your Composition

In the world of 35mm photography, editing your composition was not easy. To crop an image, you typically needed a local photo shop where you could dictate crop marks and reprint photos to your personal specifications. Or, at some photo stores, you could insert your picture into a kiosk and recompose your image on the screen and print the result minutes later. Of course, now that you have a digital camera and a PC, you don't have to drive across town and pay money to do it in a store anymore. Now you've got the tools to do it yourself at home.

Do It in Shutterfly: Cropping

Let's be honest: cropping is usually something we do right before we print or share a picture, so it makes a lot of sense to do our cropping in Shutterfly. It's a snap to do it there; just select your picture and click the Crop tab. If you know what size you plan to print your picture, click the size, and then drag the corners of the crop box around until the picture looks just the way you want it. Shutterfly will remember this crop selection when you order the print.

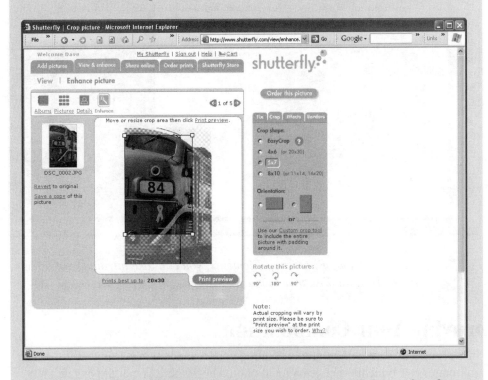

Shutterfly offers two cropping options to help you get the best prints from your images: EasyCrop and Custom Crop.

EasyCrop is designed to help you avoid undesired cropping. Unlike traditional cropping methods that subtract from your selected print area, EasyCrop allows you to select an area to print no matter what print size you choose. Shutterfly customers also have the option of cropping their images to a specific print size. By selecting this cropping option, your photos will be printed at the selected print size—without a border or padding.

1. To begin using EasyCrop, press the green View & Enhance button and navigate to a picture. (You can also navigate to the picture when you are in other parts of your account, such as Share Online and Order Prints.) Then select the green crop tab on the right.

2. Once on the cropping page, you will see your selected image with EasyCrop applied automatically. The print area you select will print at your desired print size. To preview the image, click Print Preview and then select the desired print size. To return to the cropping page, click the Return to Crop link.

3. To adjust the crop area, click a corner of the image and drag it to the desired size. To move the crop area, click in the middle of the image and drag it to the desired location.

4. To crop your image to a specific print size, first select the desired print size. You can then adjust the cropping for the image and preview the printed image.

Custom Crop allows you to crop your image to any size or shape. Your selection will be printed in its entirety with a simple white border added as padding. You can change the padding style by clicking the Borders tab and choosing one of Shutterfly's simple border styles. Because the Custom Crop option uses simple borders to pad the image, you will default back to the EasyCrop if you apply one of the decorative borders to your picture or select the Trim My Picture to Make My Border an Even Width option.

Cropping Your Image

We wouldn't be surprised if this were the single most common change made to digital photographs. Because you can crop and recompose your images so easily on the computer, there's a far-less urgent need to compose your shot perfectly in the viewfinder. Instead, you can tweak the shot to your heart's content afterwards, when you have time to think about it and try different options. In fact, the more megapixels your camera can shoot, the more cropping you can do. If you have a 2- or 3-megapixel camera and intend to mount your shot as an 8×10-inch print, you can't throw away very many pixels. But if you have a 5- or 6-megapixel camera, you can discard a fair bit of your photo and still have enough resolution to make a big print.

Here's how to do it:

1. Load an image into Paint Shop Pro. Adjust it so that you can see the entire image on screen at once. To do that, you may need the Zoom tool, shaped like a magnifying glass. Click on it, and then click on the picture with the right mouse button to shrink it, or the left button to enlarge it, until it comfortably takes up most of the screen.

TIP   *Even without using the Magnifying Glass, you can roll the scroll wheel on your mouse to change the image's zoom level.*

Crop tool

Zoom tool

2. Click on the Crop tool, shaped like the thick frame.

3. To crop the picture to a specific print size, like 5×7 or 8×10, click the Presets icon in the Tool Options palette at the top of the screen and click the print size you want. Then click OK. The crop box appears in the picture.

4. To move the crop box around within the image, move the mouse inside the box so that you see the mouse pointer change into a four-way arrow. Click and drag the box around the image.

5. To change the size of the crop box, hold the pointer over the box outline. You should see a two-way arrow. Now just click-and-drag to change the height or width of the box.

Resize crop marks

6. When your crop box represents the picture as you want it composed, click the check mark button in the Tool Options palette. The image will be immediately cropped down to size, which you can save as a new file or save to replace the older image. Compare the original and cropped versions of this karate picture:

TIP

By default, the Tool Options palette is docked to the toolbars at the top of the screen. If you don't see it, it may not be activated. Choose View | Palettes | Tool Options. It should now appear onscreen. Notice that this important dialog box changes depending upon which tool you have selected.

Rotating Your Perspective

Not all of your shots are going to be plain old, horizontal shots—especially if you took our advice in Chapter 3 and went nuts with camera position and perspective. If you have images from your camera that are sideways—you took the pictures sideways, so you have to turn your head to look at them on the PC—you should fix those images right away so it's easy to edit and share them in the right orientation. It's a snap.

Do It in Shutterfly: Rotating

6

Shutterfly lets you rotate a picture to the left or right by 90 degrees, or flip it upside down by spinning it 180 degrees—all with a single click. If you find a picture that needs to be adjusted, find the Rotate This Picture buttons under the image editing box. Just click the button that represents the rotation you need.

Some image editors, like Paint Shop Pro, even have one-click buttons for rotating your images to the left or right by 90 degrees. Here's what you need to do to fix a sideways image:

1. Load the sideways image in Paint Shop Pro and decide which way it needs to be rotated—right (clockwise) or left (counterclockwise). Let's assume we need to turn the picture clockwise.

2. Choose Image | Rotate | Rotate Clockwise 90. The image immediately spins accordingly.

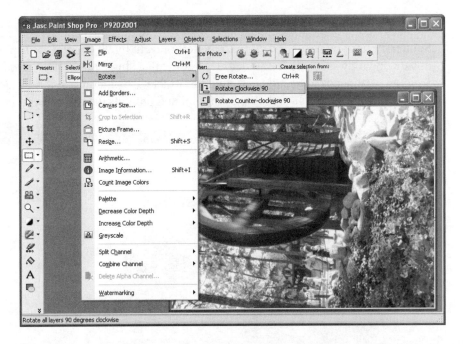

If your image editor doesn't have such a one-step rotate tool, it probably still lets you rotate by an arbitrary amount. You can even do that in Paint Shop Pro; choose Image | Rotate | Free Rotate, and then specify how much you want to rotate the image in the Free Rotate dialog box. Typically, you'd click Left or Right and make sure the button for 90 is selected, and then click OK.

3. The image should rotate such that it is oriented properly; if you made a mistake, choose Edit | Undo and try again.

There are other ways to reorient your image as well. If you took the picture with the camera upside down, for instance (and stranger things have happened, trust us), you can choose Image | Flip from the menu. Likewise, you can flip it left-to-right, giving you a mirror image of the original shot, by choosing Image | Mirror.

Leveling a Crooked Picture

There's nothing quite as annoying as a crooked picture. Especially when the horizon or some other straight line is visible in the image, a crooked shot can ruin an otherwise great picture. Even if the horizon is only off a little, it can be annoying, but you can use the principle you learned in the last section, on rotating sideways images, to fix this annoyance. Here's what you need to do:

1. Load the crooked image into Paint Shop Pro. Decide which way it needs to spin to correct the error, and estimate by how many degrees. Most errors, even seemingly egregious ones, are typically less than 2 or 3 degrees.

2. Choose Image | Rotate | Free Rotate.

3. Specify the direction (left or right) and enter a number in the Degrees box. You can type in a decimal, such as **.5** (which is half of a degree), if you want. Click OK to see the result.

4. Inspect the result. If you aren't satisfied, choose Edit | Undo and try again with a different angle of rotation. When you are happy, save the file.

> **TIP** *If there's a straight line in your picture—like a building or the horizon, try using the straightening tool instead. Paint Shop Pro, like most image editors, lets you lay the straightening tool on a line that is supposed to be vertical or horizontal, and the picture is automatically reoriented to that line. It's a fast way to adjust your picture.*

When you're done rotating your image, you may need to crop it down a bit, because the rotation probably introduced some unwanted background color in the corners of your picture.

Improve the Color and Brightness in Your Image

Some of these edits require the most artistic skill, so we saved them for last. Honestly, changing color to black-and-white can be accomplished in a snap, but fixing elements of your picture like bad color or poor exposure will take some practice before you can make your images really look right. But don't worry about that; time in your image editor is free, and if you stick with it, you can fix some badly mangled shots!

Fixing the Color Balance

Ask a serious photographer what is most frustrating about digital imaging, and you'll get a short list of major gripes: the shutter lag when taking pictures, limited dynamic range, and goofy color balance—in other words, pictures that turn out too blue or red. We've already talked a bit about some of these shortcomings. Often, your digital camera will miscalculate your color balance and give you an image with a pronounced color cast. What does that mean? Not only won't there be a true white or black in your picture, but all the other colors will be a bit off as well.

Thankfully, you can fix the color balance of your photos in almost any image editor. In Paint Shop Pro, load an image with something of a color cast and locate a part of your image with pure white or black, and then zoom in on it. Next, choose Adjust | Color Balance | Black and White Points. The Black and White Points dialog should appear. Assuming you want to use a white region of the image to correct your photo, click on the rightmost dropper in the dialog box, directly above the white color box (you could use black instead, if you want to).

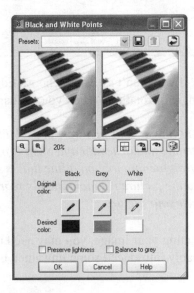

Do It in Shutterfly: Color Adjustments

Click the Effects tab and you'll get access to a handful of cool tools you can apply to your picture. You can only do one per picture—you can't apply both black and white and soft focus, for instance—but this tab makes it easy to saturate the colors in a picture or add a sepia effect.

To change the color saturation, click Saturate, and then click a position in the adjustment area to change the level of saturation. You need to click where you want the slider to go. Moving the slider to the right increases the color saturation, while moving the slider to the left drains the color out of your picture. Check out the color section of this book for a peek at how these various effects can change your pictures.

6

Should you change the colors in your picture using the Effects tab, you'll probably want to turn off VividPics, which automatically enhances your picture when printed. To do that, click Don't Apply Automatic Corrections to Picture on the left side of the screen.

Click the dropper in your image, directly in the white region. Preview the change, and, if you like the results, click OK to save your changes.

Incidentally, the process in Photoshop Elements is very similar. To open the white point control, choose Enhance | Color | Color Cast. You don't need to specify white or black in Elements; the program will figure it out. Just click in the image and click OK to accept the changes to your image's color balance.

Brightening Gloomy Shots

Everyone has a stockpile of too-dark images. The flash didn't reach the subject, or perhaps the camera underexposed the subject because of a bright background. Back in the first part of the book, we told you how to avoid those kinds of problems when you take the picture, but you can also repair some of the damage in postprocessing.

There are three primary ways of adjusting the brightness in an image:

- **You can use the Brightness control.** Brightness raises or lowers the entire image's brightness indiscriminately, whether all areas need it or not. On the other hand, if just one portion of an image needs to be brightened, you use a Selection tool to isolate just the part of the picture that needs fixing, and then add brightness. When part of an image is selected, operations you perform on the image occur in the selected region.

TIP   *Use the Selection tool to add or remove brightness only where it's needed.*

- **Alternately, you can use the Gamma control.** *Gamma* is a tool that affects the midtones of an image more than the extreme bright and dark regions; that means you can brighten a dark skin tone without washing out a dark shadow nearby. Gamma affects a limited range of brightness in the image, so you can better target your changes. We think gamma almost always works better than brightness.

- **Finally, the best way to tweak the brightness of an image is by inspecting the histogram.** This is a graphical display that tells you the distribution of light and dark pixels in an image, and can be a powerful way to correct your shots—as long as you're willing to invest a little time to learn how to use it. We'll show you the histogram a bit later.

Correcting with Brightness and Contrast

Let's start with the brightness and contrast controls. The process for changing brightness in an image is similar regardless of software, but we'll use Paint Shop Pro, as usual, for our example. Here's the general procedure:

1. Load the offending image into Paint Shop Pro.

2. Choose Adjust | Brightness and Contrast | Brightness/Contrast. The Brightness and Contrast dialog box appears.

3. Use the Brightness slider to adjust the image. You can see the effect of the change in your image immediately by clicking on the Proof button, which is shaped like an eye. Auto Proof, to the left of the Proof button, leaves proofing on all the time, so updates are made constantly as you work the slider.

4. Typically, you'll also need to change the contrast in proportion to the brightness to keep the image from getting washed out. Experiment until you see the result you want.

5. When you're satisfied with the results, click OK. Your image will be updated with the new brightness value.

Better Corrections with Gamma

As we mentioned, the Gamma control is often a better remedy for fixing an overly dark or overly bright image. We've found it's often the midtones in a picture that need enhancement, and brightness tends to wash out dark regions and increase the intensity of the highlights, overexposing them. The Gamma control, on the other hand, doesn't affect the brightest and darkest parts of an image, so you can't wash out shadows with this tool, for instance. So as a general rule, you should see if gamma gets the job done.

To tweak the gamma, just choose Adjust | Brightness and Contrast | Gamma Correction, and move the sliders (the Link control keeps all three colors in sync, which is the most common way to use this tool). Unless your image is very poorly exposed, you shouldn't need to change the gamma value above 1.5 or below .5.

Fine-Tuning Images with the Histogram

The most precise and powerful way of correcting your images is with the histogram. The *histogram* is a graph that shows the relative amount of information stored in each color channel in your image; or, in plain English, it displays how many pixels are dark and light in your image. The left side of the graph represents the darkest part of the image, while the right side is the lightest. A graph like the one on the left in Figure 6-2 has a lot of midtones, while the one on the right is mostly filled with dark pixels. We can use that information to tweak the brightness and contrast.

TIP   *Tweaking the histogram only takes a few seconds and can improve many of your shots.*

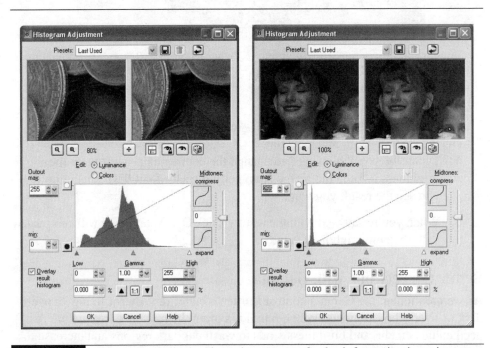

FIGURE 6-2   Histograms tell a lot about the amount of color information in an image.

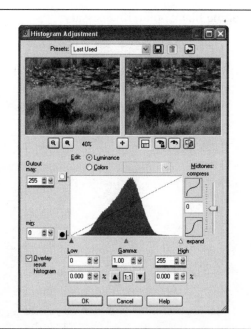

FIGURE 6-3   The Histogram Adjustment tool is a precise way to adjust brightness and contrast.

Most good image editing programs—like Paint Shop Pro, PhotoShop, and Photoshop Elements—have a handy tool for adjusting the light levels in your image using the histogram chart and a few sliders. In Paint Shop Pro, it's found at Adjust | Brightness and Contrast | Histogram Adjustment. If you're using the full version of Photoshop, it's found in Image | Adjust | Levels. Finally, Adobe Photoshop Elements puts this control in Enhance | Brightness/Contrast | Levels.

No matter which program you use, this tool works more or less the same way. You simply want to move the sliders under the histogram to set the white and black points, stretching and optimizing the distribution of brightness information in the image. Paint Shop Pro throws in a Gamma control into the same dialog box, which is treated separately (as the Curves tool) in Photoshop.

Suppose you have an image like the one in Figure 6-3. Here's how you would correct the image using the Histogram Adjustment in Paint Shop Pro:

1. Because the histogram curve drops off before reaching the right side of the graph, that tells us that there are few pixels with very bright colors. As a consequence, you should drag the white point slider to the left to meet the point where the graph really ends. That sets this point in the image as white, and should brighten the image. You should see the graph stretch as you drag the end points.

2. Do the same for the black point, if necessary.

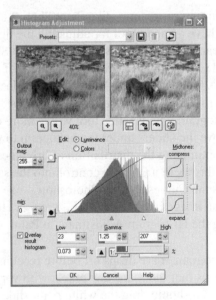

3. Now use the gamma slider, if needed, to adjust the overall brightness level in the image's midtones.

Adding Snap to Your Colors

There are a few ways to add life to washed-out, flat, or bland pictures. One way is to use the Contrast control. Because bland pictures are often a result of low contrast, you can increase the contrast in the image and make the scene look much "punchier." To do that, simply find the Contrast control and work the slider. In Paint Shop Pro, you can find the contrast in Adjust | Brightness and Contrast | Brightness/Contrast.

> **TIP** *While we often want to increase contrast to improve a picture, you can do interesting things by lowering contrast as well. Want to create some artificial fog? Just reduce the contrast in a picture by about 50 percent, and the image seems obscured by a dense fog.*

Another way to improve your image is with the Saturation tool. *Saturation* increases or decreases the intensity of colors in an image, much like the saturation control on your television. Too much saturation can make the picture look like it was taken on Mars, but it can add life to an otherwise bland picture.

> **TIP** *Do you have a people picture that's a little too red? This doesn't happen often, but it can occur when you take indoor pictures in artificial light. Back off on the saturation slightly to get a more natural skin tone.*

In Paint Shop Pro, the Saturation control is found in Adjust | Hue and Saturation | Hue/Saturation/ Lightness. Experiment with the Saturation tool—it's fun. You can bleach all the color out of your picture by reducing the saturation to zero, for instance, or hyperactivate the colors by going in the other direction.

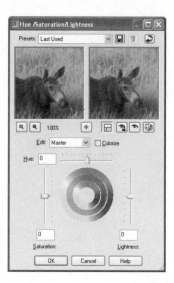

TIP

Don't forget that programs like Paint Shop Pro also have automatic controls for many of these tweaks. You can find an automatic contrast adjustment as well as an autosaturation tool under the Enhance Photo button in the toolbar.

Brightness Only Goes So Far

You need to know the ugly little secret of brightness and Gamma control. You can only take it so far, because you can't add detail to an image that wasn't there when you originally took the picture. A black shadow, for instance, will only become gray as you continue to increase brightness—you'll never see the authentic Bigfoot creature that was hiding in the thicket of trees. That's why it's important to start with the best exposure you can, although you can always try enhancing it afterwards. You can sometimes salvage an otherwise throwaway image.

Chapter 7

Cleaning Up
Your Images

In this chapter you'll learn to...

- Sharpen blurry images

- Blur the background to enhance apparent sharpness

- Use the painting tools in your image editor

- Remove ugly red eye from flash photos

- Eliminate distracting objects with airbrushing

- Repair tears and scratches on photos

- Create a panorama from a series of photos

In the last chapter, we looked at easy and fast techniques you can use to gussy up your images—stuff like how to rotate or resize your images, correct bad colors, and even save them in different file formats.

But there's so much more that you can do. In this chapter, we'll go one step beyond and learn how to fix your images with techniques that change reality. You'll see how to remove red eye caused by flash photography, how to sharpen (or blur) a picture, and how to airbrush away distracting elements from a scene and move elements around within a picture.

This chapter is filled with techniques that sit between what we would call elementary quick changes and special effects. We're not adding Elvis to your holiday pictures, but we're certainly going beyond color correction. Strap in and have fun with your images and your favorite image editor!

Sharpening Blurry Pictures

We know what you're thinking. Wow! I can sharpen my blurry pictures! Technology is great!

Well, let us begin by saying that as great as digital imaging is, you can never add detail or information into a picture that wasn't there to begin with. That's why we're always amused by movies in which a spy takes a surveillance videotape and enlarges the image enough to read the phone number on a piece of paper across the room. No matter how much they enlarge images in the movies, those Hollywood computers always seem to sharpen the focus perfectly.

With that said, there is some hope for your *slightly* blurry images. There are two ways to sharpen an image: a direct way, using the Sharpen tool in your image editing program, and an indirect way, which amounts to blurring the background so your subject doesn't look quite so bad. Let's see how to do both.

TIP

As you may have guessed, you can combine those two techniques.

Using the Sharpen Filter to Enhance Your Picture

The easiest way to sharpen an image is with the Sharpen tool. This tool increases the contrast between pixels, making the image seem sharper, as you can see by looking at Figure 7-1. If you tried taking a picture while riding a roller coaster, though, no amount of sharpening will restore sharp focus.

In most graphics programs, a few different kinds of sharpening filters are available. These are the most common options:

- **Sharpening**   This affects all the pixels in your image indiscriminately. Sharpen More is a common alternative, which is just somewhat more intense.

- **Edge Sharpening**   This effect only increases the contrast along edges in your picture, where a lack of sharpness is most obvious. It is usually more effective than Sharpening, and it is less damaging to the rest of the image.

- **Unsharp Mask**   This variation of Edge Sharpening adjusts the contrast of pixels that neighbor an edge in addition to the edge itself. This is the most common sharpening filter, and, in fact, it's pretty standard practice for photographers to run the Unsharp Mask filter on most pictures that they plan to print.

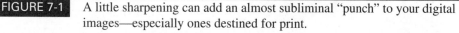

FIGURE 7-1   A little sharpening can add an almost subliminal "punch" to your digital images—especially ones destined for print.

In Paint Shop Pro, the Sharpen, Sharpen More, and Unsharp Mask filters are available from the Adjust I Sharpness menu.

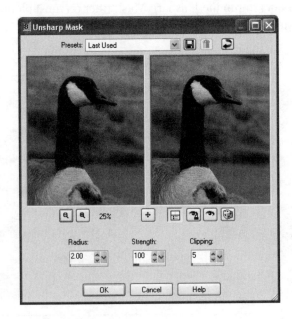

Which one of those options should you use? Not all programs offer all three filters, but if you have a choice, Edge Sharpening is almost always more effective than the plain old Sharpening filter. And Unsharp Mask works best of all, but it takes a little tweaking on your part. You'll generally get to set at least three options, as you can see here:

- **Strength**   Sometimes called Amount, this is the intensity of the sharpening effect.

- **Radius**   This determines how many pixels around the edges are also affected by the filter.

- **Clipping**   Also called Threshhold, this determines how different the pixels need to be before they're considered an edge.

TIP   *Start with 100 for Strength and 1.0 for Radius, and watch the way the filter changes as you change Clipping. A Clipping of 0 is the most harsh effect; beyond about 30, changing Clipping has no real effect on your image. Likewise, raising Radius beyond 1.5 rarely has an attractive effect on your image.*

Blur to Sharpen

Using the Sharpening filter is certainly one way to make your image look sharper, but there's another, more subtle and more "artistic" way to enhance the apparent

How to ...   Undo a Big Mistake

Paint Shop Pro, like many image editors, has an extensive undo history you can use to fix a major boo-boo. If you spend ten minutes making edits to a photo and you don't want to choose Edit | Undo 25 times in a row to get rid of it all, do this:

1. Choose Edit | Command History. You'll see a dialog box that lists all the operations you've performed, from the last back to the first (reverse chronological order).

2. Scroll down until you find the point at which your unwanted edits begin.

3. Click that first unwanted edit. All the operations from there back to the last operation you performed become highlighted.

4. Click Undo. The image will revert to an earlier state.

sharpness of your image—blur the background. This process works best when you're taking a picture in which the subject is distinct from the background, like a family portrait.

To blur the background of your image, you'll need to isolate the subject so the blurring only happens in the rest of the picture. Once your subject is selected, you need to invert the selection so that the Blur filter happens to everything except the subject. Finally, you can run the Blur filter on your image. In Paint Shop Pro, you can find Blur by choosing an option from the Effects | Blur menu. Once you've blurred your background, turn off the selection and save your image.

That's the quick overview. Here's how to pull off this feat of digital trickery:

1. Load a slightly blurry portrait that you'd like to sharpen into Paint Shop Pro.

2. Select the Freehand tool and set it to Smart Edge. Set the Feather value to about 5—that way the transition from the subject to the background won't be abrupt.

3. Trace the outline of the subject's face or body, being careful to stay along the edge.

4. When you have completely selected the subject, choose Adjust | Sharpness | Unsharp Mask to sharpen the subject, but not affect the background.

Simulating a Shallow Depth of Field

Let's say that you wanted to take a picture with a sharp foreground and a fuzzy background, but your automatic camera settings didn't cooperate and the entire picture turned out sharp overall. Well, it's easy to simulate the out-of-focus effect that a wide-open aperture gives your background by using the select-invert-blur technique we used to give the subject more apparent sharpness. You'll need to heap on liberal amounts of blur for this technique to work. You can run the Blur filter several times until you get the effect you like.

5. Next, choose Selections | Invert from the menu. This "flips" the selection so the subject isn't selected, but everything else is.

6. Choose Adjust | Blur | Blur More. You should see the background blur slightly. If you're not happy with the result, blur it again. In fact, you can repeatedly use the blur effect until the background is sufficiently blurred.

7. Finally, when the image is complete, choose Selections | Select None.

We hope the subject now looks better, especially in comparison to the background. Compare the two images in Figure 7-2, for instance, for a look at this effect in action.

FIGURE 7-2   Blurring the background can simulate a shallow depth of field—great for portraits—while also giving the impression of a sharper subject.

Painting on Your Pictures

Some of the techniques you use to edit digital photos require a little, well . . . painting. And if you take a look at your image editor—especially a full-featured one like Paint Shop Pro or Adobe PhotoShop—you'll see a complete set of painting tools. These digital gadgets let you change the colors in an image on a pixel-by-pixel basis. How do they do that? Take a look at Table 7-1; there you can see the most important tools in Paint Shop Pro's Paint toolbar. These are fairly typical tools as image editors go; you'll find their equivalent in most other programs.

NOTE
Paint Shop Pro stores several tools in each slot of the toolbar. Click the arrow next to each tool to see all the available options.

Repairing the Evil Eye

The easiest way to avoid red eye is to keep it out of your pictures to begin with—by using the Red Eye Reduction mode on your digital camera or not using the flash in a dark room. Red eye, of course, is the phenomenon that occurs when the camera flash reflects off the subject's retina, because the pupils are wide open in a dark room. If you've got red eye, either because you didn't take the necessary precautions or because you've just scanned an old picture that has red eye, you can correct it on the PC fairly easily.

Removing Red Eye Using an Image Editor

Check to see if your image editing software has an automatic red eye removal feature. Some red eye removal software is completely automated. Paint Shop Pro, for instance, has a great semiautomated process for eliminating red eye:

1. Open a photo that includes someone with a case of Evil Eye.

2. From the menu, choose Adjust | Red-eye Removal. You'll see the Red-eye Removal dialog box.

Tool	Description
	Pan. This tool is used to move image windows around within Paint Shop Pro. It's a safe default setting to use because it won't do anything to your image if you click in the picture.
	Zoom. Zoom into the image by left-clicking; zoom out by right-clicking.
	Crop. It lets you cut out unwanted bits of your picture.
	Selection. It lets you select portions of an image for further editing.
	Freehand. This is another way to select portions of an image.
	Magic Wand. This tool selects a region for editing based on color. Because photos have lots of similar colors, you can click on a region and the wand will select everything nearby that's a similar color. It's an easy way to select a person's face, for instance.
	Dropper. This tool determines the color of the currently selected pixel and makes that the current foreground color for painting and editing.
	Color Replacer. This great painting tool puts the power of many of the program's effects—like brightness and hue changes, effects filters, and more—into a brush so you can paint them on.
	Paint Brush. This is just what it sounds like. It lets you paint on the image, not unlike the way you'd paint with a real brush. It's a lot more flexible than a real brush, though, because you can change features like the size and shape of the brush, as well as the amount of paint that you can spread at once.
	Airbrush. You can configure this tool to splatter paint on your image like an airbrush.
	Clone Brush. This tool lets you paint with pixels found elsewhere in your image, effectively cloning a part of your picture as you paint.
	Scratch Remover. This automated tool erases scratches from scanned photographs.
	Eraser. This tool lets you paint with the currently selected foreground and background colors.
	Flood Fill. Pours paint into a region. The currently selected color will run right up to whatever color edges exist. Like the Magic Wand, you can set the color tolerance.
	Text. This tool lets you write text anywhere in your image, in any color and any font.
	Pen. Use this tool to draw straight and curved lines in your image.

TABLE 7-1 Highlights from the Paint Tools Palette in Paint Shop Pro

Where the Controls Are

Of course, every camera's controls are a bit different, so we can't show you exactly how to operate yours. But many models are similar. Throughout the book, we use the Canon PowerShot A75, Olympus Stylus A410, and Sony CyberShot DSC-L1 as a guide to using your own camera.

Set the Flash to Red Eye Reduction Mode

If you have a camera like the Canon PowerShot A75, Red Eye mode is controlled just by pushing the up arrow on the control dial on the back of the camera. Every time you push up, the flash changes to the next mode. Red eye reduction is turned on when you see, in the digital display, the eye icon next to the flash icon lit up.

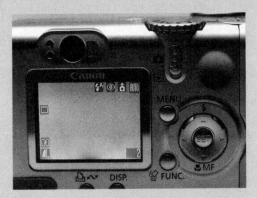

On the Olympus Stylus 410, the right button (with the flash symbol next to it) cycles you through the various flash modes. Press it until you see the eye icon appear on the digital display.

The Sony Cyber-shot DSC-L1 buries the red eye reduction control in the menu system. Press the menu button and push the joystick control to the right until you enter the Setup menu. Then nudge it right again and arrow down until you reach Red Eye Reduction. If it is currently set to Off, arrow right, and then up to choose On. Push the stick in to make the selection and press menu a second time to save your changes.

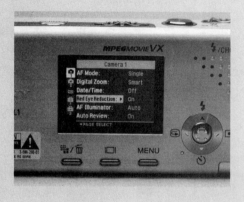

7

3. Move the image on the right around by dragging it with the mouse pointer until you see a red eye in the middle of the frame. (Don't try dragging the left side around, because that's where you "draw" eyes.) Once you can see the eye, zoom in until it fills much of the frame.

Do It in Shutterfly: Remove Red Eye

You can easily remove red eye in Shutterfly. Open a picture in Shutterfly and click the green Fix tab on the right. Then click on one of the eyes you need to correct and you'll see an enlarged version of the eye in the box on the right. Click in the center of the eye. If you like the change, click Save Fix. Continue this until you are satisfied with the correction.

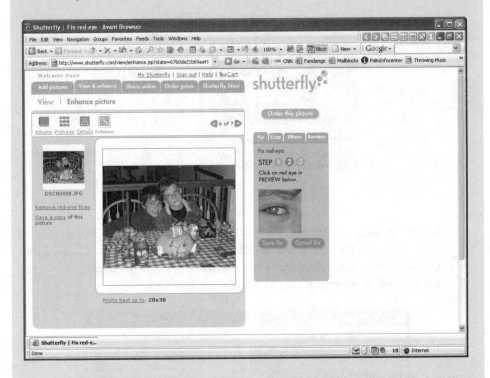

Now click on another eye to fix and repeat the process. You can fix as many eyes as you need using this process—if you don't like what you see, just click Cancel Fix to undo one eye, or click the Remove Red-Eye Fixes link to undo both, at once.

4. Make sure that the Method is Auto Human Eye and select the proper hue for the person you're correcting. Then pick an eye color. Once everything is ready, click in the dead-center of a red eye and drag the mouse away from the center until you've covered the red with the new eye. You can resize and reposition the eye if needed.

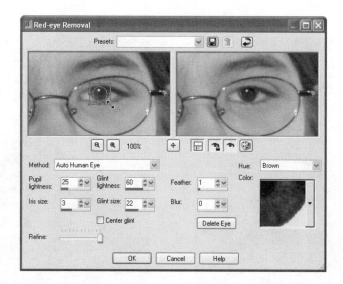

5. Repeat the process for the other eye. When both eyes are finished, click OK to close the Red-eye Removal dialog box and keep your changes.

Airbrushing Away Distractions

Have you ever taken a great landscape shot only to realize—far too late to reshoot the picture—that a telephone pole is in the middle of what should be a serene scene? Or found a tourist in a loud shirt standing right behind your family in a picture that you wanted to frame? Don't worry—this section will show you how to eliminate those kinds of distractions with a little digital airbrushing.

The tool at the heart of this magical process is the Clone tool. This handy feature, found in most image editors, lets you copy pixels from one region of your image to another. That means you can "airbrush away" distracting aspects of a picture—like power lines, hotspots, tourists, and so on—by duplicating a similar or nearby part of the image (see Figure 7-3). Typically, smaller and more isolated distractions are easier to airbrush away than larger ones (or objects that cut through the main part of your picture); but if you're patient, you can get great results from a surprising number of photos that you thought you'd have to throw away.

To use the Clone tool in Paint Shop Pro, just do this:

1. Click on the Clone tool in the tool palette. It looks like a pair of paintbrushes.

2. You'll need to find a region in your image that is similar to the area you want to cover. If you want to airbrush away a power line that runs through the air, for instance, you can look for a nearby patch of sky similar enough that you can paint over the power line with this other section of sky.

FIGURE 7-3   Paint away distractions with the Clone tool.

3. Set the source for your cloning operation. In Paint Shop Pro, just position the mouse pointer over the area you're going to steal color from and either right-click or hold the SHIFT key and click.

4. Move your mouse over to the area you want to airbrush and start painting. Don't try to cover the blemish all at once. Paint a little, pick up the mouse, and paint again. This reduces the chances that a recognizable pattern will appear as a result of your painting.

The Clone tool works best in small areas, because you can start to tell that something is wrong with the area you're cloning to if you paint over too large a region.

> **NOTE** *The Clone tool has two different modes. In one mode, when you pick up the brush and paint elsewhere, the source stays where you put it: this is called* nonaligned. *If you pick up the brush and start painting elsewhere, and the source moves the same relative distance from where you first started, this is the* aligned *mode. Some pictures work better with one mode or the other. Experiment to see which is best in each situation.*

By the way: there's another way to solve this problem. If your blemish is small enough, just try using your image editor's Scratch Remover tool. It won't give you good results all the time (sometimes it'll look like the picture is "smeared" around the area where the tool did its work), but often it's the fastest, one-step way to improve your photo.

Cleaning Up Old and Damaged Pictures

An unexpected benefit of digital imaging and editing has been the capability to restore old pictures—heirlooms and keepsakes that you may have written off as too badly damaged to be of much value anymore. Some of the techniques we've already mentioned can be used to fix these old prints on your PC. First, of course, you'll need to scan these images into the PC. You can get a good quality flatbed scanner very inexpensively these days—for under $100, in fact. If the pictures you want to scan are slides or negatives, you'll need a scanner with something called a transparency adapter, which is a little adapter for the scanner with a backlight that illuminates those old formats. After you have the hardware, you'll want to scan your old prints at the highest resolution your scanner makes available—that'll make it easier to print them later. From there, it's just a matter of applying digital editing techniques to repair them.

Removing Picture Scratches

It's a common tale: after a bad moving experience, you find that one of your irreplaceable wedding pictures became the victim of nasty scratches. Thankfully, your image editor can help you fix it. You can take several approaches to fix scratches, depending upon where they are in the image, how prominent the scratches are, and their relative size with respect to the rest of the image:

- In some cases, you can select and copy an undamaged area of the picture that is similar in color and overall texture to the damaged portion, and then paste it over the damaged area with a liberal amount of feathering to smooth the edges. This is particularly effective in fairly uniform backgrounds, such as the sky.

- Another alternative—and the more common solution—is to use the cloning tool (see the earlier section, "Airbrushing Away Distractions," for more details). Select the cloning tool and use a nearby, similar, but undamaged section of the image to paint over the mark. Remember to use short, dabbing motions to paint, or you'll introduce an undesirable pattern into the image.

- You can use the automated scratch remover found in many image editors. Paint Shop Pro's Scratch Remover (it looks like a trowel) lets you drag a selection box over a long, straight scratch. It then removes the scratch by painting over it with nearby colors automatically. This technique doesn't work well for wide scratches or scratches that curve or bend—it's off to the Clone tool for those.

Removing Dust, Dirt, and Digital Noise

Your images can be filled with little specks that come from grainy, high-speed 35mm film, from bad scans, or from using a digital camera in very low light. Whatever the reason you get specks on your image, most image editors have a Despeckle tool. In Paint Shop Pro, you can find it at Adjust | Add/Remove Noise | Despeckle.

Making a Panoramic Photo

A *panorama* is an image that's wider than the ordinary images produced by your camera, such as the one in Figure 7-4.

Panoramas are typically used to take landscapes, because they provide the wide, sweeping vistas that look so impressive. They're great for capturing eye-popping pictures of your vacation spots. You can take a panorama of anything, though—a school play, the inside of your home, or some other scene. The key to making something into a panorama with a digital camera is that you'll need to take two or more images and "stitch" them together on your PC. So, if you're taking a landscape, for instance, the same cars, people, and other objects shouldn't move much as you rotate your camera and take successive shots.

| FIGURE 7-4 | You can connect a number of images to make a wide (or tall) panoramic shot. |

7

There are two steps to taking a panorama: photographing the scene and stitching the images together afterward. When shooting the pictures, keep these tips in mind:

- You'll need to take a series of pictures that overlap. Try to get 30 percent–50 percent of each image to overlap into the next picture to make it easier to stitch them together. Scenes with lots of movement are a poor candidate for panoramas, because the computer needs to look for similar regions in common from one picture to another. A little movement is fine, but the overall scene should be essentially static.

- To keep each image's perspective identical, you'll need to take all the pictures from the same location. Don't drift a few feet forward, backward, or to the left or right as you photograph. Ideally, you might even want to take the shots on a tripod, but we've gotten awesome results just holding the camera in our hands.

- Avoid zooming all the way out to wide-angle, because this can distort the images and make it difficult to line up edges. Zoom in about halfway between wide angle and telephoto.

Now it's time to make the panorama. There's a hard way and an easy way; which way you choose depends upon how much enthusiasm you have for delicate editing and how much money you have to spend on yet another image editing program.

If you're game for doing it the easy way—and that's the method I highly, highly recommend—you need to purchase a panorama program that automates the entire process for you. Several programs are around that do the stitching for you. If you're interested, check out any of these:

- Microsoft Digital Image Suite

- Adobe Photoshop Elements

- Jasc Paint Shop Photo Album

- Ulead Cool 360

- ArcSoft Panorama Maker

Using any of those programs, all you need to do is drag-and-drop the individual images in the proper order. In fact, Microsoft's Digital Image Suite doesn't even require that—the software automatically figures out what order the pictures should go in.

The software matches the edges all by itself, and creates a panorama that you can save as a regular digital image.

The Resolution Advantage

Not all panoramas are photographed just to take wide, scenic landscapes. Sometimes, you might want to photograph a subject in sections, so you can get more pixels to make a high-res print.

What am I talking about? Consider a situation in which you want to make a 20×30-inch poster-sized print, but your 2-megapixel camera doesn't have enough resolution to make a sharp picture that large. You can still get the shot, as long as you're trying to photograph a stationary object. Shoot it in sections, and then stitch the individual segments together on the PC using a program that lets you create a panorama out of a grid of horizontal and vertical images. When you're done, you'll end up with a much higher-resolution image because it'll have a lot more pixels than a single photo would have. And you can make a poster from that. Figure 7-5 shows how we took six sequential photos of a car—each one measuring about 2 megapixels—and ended up with a huge, super high-resolution 8 megapixel shot that's plenty big for just about any print you could possibly want to make.

FIGURE 7-5   You can stitch several smaller images together to make a huge print.

Make a Virtual Reality Panorama

The panoramas we've talked about so far are very wide or tall images that go beyond the ordinary aspect ratio people expect to see when they look at a picture—that's what helps make them look so striking. You have another option entirely.

Perhaps you've seen virtual reality movies on the Web or in online encyclopedias like Encarta. They present a scene in a small window that, when you click-and-drag the mouse inside, spins around so you can see a full 360 degrees, as if you were there. When you think about it, isn't that just a 360-degree panorama in which you only see a small piece at once? Indeed, that's the secret behind these VR movies. And that means there's nothing particularly magical about them. You can make

Do It in Shutterfly: Print a Panorama

The great thing about panoramas is that they often have plenty of pixels for making poster size prints. If you stitch several pictures into a panorama, for instance, you can print it as a 20×30-inch print. Because your panorama will be much longer than it is tall, though, you may have to trim your print down to size after it arrives. Much of the print will be white space with a narrow print running through the middle, like a widescreen movie on a square television. The panorama posters are printed on heavier paper, though, to resist wear, and they are delivered in mailing tubes for protection.

your own VR movies and share them in e-mail or on the Web. The most common format for these interactive panoramas is Apple's QuickTime, as seen in the following illustration.

To make your own VR movies, you'll need to take a series of images that can be assembled into a complete 360-degree panorama. You'll also need special panorama software. The best—and most affordable—programs that we've found are Ulead's Cool 360 and ArcSoft Panorama Maker. Both of these excellent programs let you create panoramas and save them in QuickTime format, which most people can view on their computers without any additional software (if they don't already have QuickTime installed, it's available free from Apple's web site). Panorama Maker even has an option to let you save your VR movie as a web page, which makes it easier to post on the Web.

Improving Your Sky

If you browse through your photos, you may find that many of your outdoor photos lack a certain punch—the sky is washed out, cloudless, or otherwise just a little boring.

There's a good reason for that. When you compose a photograph, you usually concentrate on the primary subject and pay little heed to the sky itself. Because the sky is a lot brighter than your subject, the camera overexposes it and your sky ends up looking at least a little bleached. Even if the sky is properly exposed, it sometimes just doesn't cooperate, and you'll have a cloudless, boring sky that doesn't match the mood you were trying to get. By adding some snap back into your skies, you can dramatically improve your so-so photos.

Multiply Your Sky

The easiest way to fix a bleached sky is to "multiply" it. What does that mean? Well, we're going to open a photo, select the sky, and copy it the clipboard. Then we'll paste copies of the sky back into the image, using a seldom-used tool to "multiply" the colors in each layer of sky to produce deeper, darker colors. If even a little blue is peeking through your sky, this technique is ideal, because it's so easy to do.

For starters, find a picture with a weak sky, perhaps like the following one. Skies rarely come more anemic than this one, so let's see what we can do with it. Open it in Paint Shop Pro.

Now try these steps:

1. Click on the Magic Wand tool in preparation for selecting the sky. The Magic Wand is one of our favorite selection tools because it grabs parts of the photo that share similar colors. Set the tolerance in the Tools Options dialog box to about 20.

2. Click the Magic Wand squarely in the middle of the sky: you should see selection marks appear around a big blotch of sky. Use the SHIFT key and click all around the sky until you've selected the entire thing, without also grabbing any non-sky parts of the picture.

3. Make sure that you've selected the entire sky—you can zoom in and pan around the image to double-check. When you know you've gotten it all, copy the selected sky to the clipboard by choosing Edit | Copy from the menu.

4. Next, choose Edit | Paste | As New Layer. You can tell two copies of the sky are in the picture because you can grab the top sky layer and drag it around. Position the new sky so it lines up perfectly with the original sky underneath.

5. Now for the magic trick that makes all this effort worthwhile: the multiply effect. Choose Layers | Properties from the menu and you'll see the Layer Properties dialog box. Set the Blend mode to Multiply. Click OK.

As soon as the dialog box disappears, you should see the colors in your sky immediately deepen. If you don't think that was enough of a change to suit you, don't worry. Here's where your artistic judgment comes in: because the sky is already copied into your clipboard, you can continue to paste new layers of sky into your image until you get the deep and colorful effect you're looking for. Using this technique, you can transform an anemic, pale blue sky into an angry, stormy scene in minutes.

CAUTION *Every time you paste in a new layer, be sure to set the blend for that new layer to Multiply, or the added layers will have no effect on the color of the sky.*

Replace the Sky

The multiply technique is not the only way to punch up a lame sky. You can also steal the sky from another photo, as we'll show you how to do now.

For starters, though, you're going to need a great photo of the sky. When we see a pretty blue sky, a swirling, cloudy day, a stormy afternoon, or a beautiful sunset, we often grab a camera and start shooting. If you fill the entire frame with sky, you'll capture all the color and intensity that you see through the viewfinder in the final image.

Shoot your sky shots with your camera's highest resolution, because you never know what resolution you'll eventually need. You might also want to take some pictures in Landscape mode and others in Portrait mode, so you have a selection of skies for any situation. Store your collection of sky images in a special folder, and you'll always have options available when you want to replace a bland sky.

Evicting the Old Sky

Ready to try this technique? Load a picture with a weak sky in Paint Shop Pro. Then follow these steps:

1. Just like last time, use the Magic Wand with the Tolerance set at a moderate level (like 20) to select the sky in the photo.

2. After the sky is completely selected, choose Selections | Invert from the menu. You should see that the foreground is now selected and the sky is not selected.

3. Copy the selected foreground to the clipboard by choosing Edit | Copy from the menu.

4. Check the image's resolution by choosing Image | Image Information from the menu. If you need to, write it down. You'll need that information in a few steps.

5. Open the image with the substitute sky in Paint Shop Pro.

6. Choose Image | Resize from the menu and fill in the proper numbers in the Pixel Size boxes to resize this image to match the original.

7. Making sure the new image is still selected, choose Edit | Paste | As New Layer from the menu. You should see the foreground from the old picture appear in the new sky photo.

8. Drag the image around as needed until it's positioned properly in the frame. If you like the results, save the new image. You're done!

Chapter 8

Sharing Your Pictures

In this chapter you'll learn to...

- ■ Share images using Shutterfly

- ■ Send and receive images via e-mail

- ■ Choose the right file format for e-mailing pictures

- ■ Compress images for e-mail and disk

- ■ Show off pictures on a handheld PC

- ■ Display images on a digital picture frame

Taking pictures is one thing; sharing them with friends, family, and coworkers is something else entirely. Of course, this is one area where your digital camera has a leg up on film cameras. To share traditional prints with someone, you need to physically give them a copy. Before digital photography, that meant visiting the photo finisher and having duplicates made.

Digital camera images are just bits and bytes of data, and that makes sharing a whole lot easier. Want to share your images? Sure, you can send them prints. But you can share them using Shutterfly or choose to e-mail them directly, yourself. Or you can show them off with a digital picture frame or on a handheld device. We'll show you how to easily make your images available to other people.

Sharing Images on the Internet with Shutterfly

Of course, you can design your own web site to help you stay connected with friends and family, and tools are around to help you do just that. But, if you're like us and you're not really thrilled by the idea of learning how to use a web page design program, there's an easier solution—one that requires no programming, no eye for page design, and no Internet skills. The solution? Post your pictures on Shutterfly and your friends and family will receive a personal e-mail from you and a URL link, which connects them to an online slide show of your snapshots.

Sharing your pictures on Shutterfly lets you invite specific friends and family to view just the images you want them to see. (Pictures in shared albums are not available to the general public.) Shutterfly share recipients can even order prints and products if they wish. And that way, they get just the photos they want, and you can save yourself the steps of ordering and mailing pictures for them.

To share a set of pictures on Shutterfly, do this:

1. Click the Share online tab at the top of the Shutterfly web page.

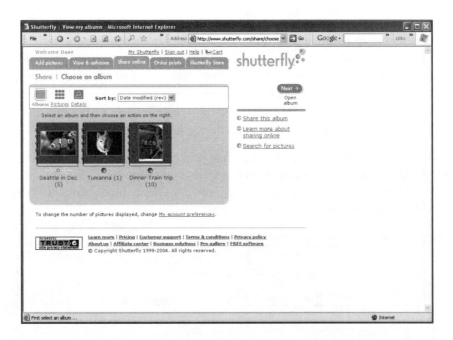

2. Click an album that has pictures you want to share.

3. When the album is open, click on the check box under each picture that you want to share. The check box will be checked, indicating that it's ready to share. You can share as many pictures as you like—just one or the entire album.

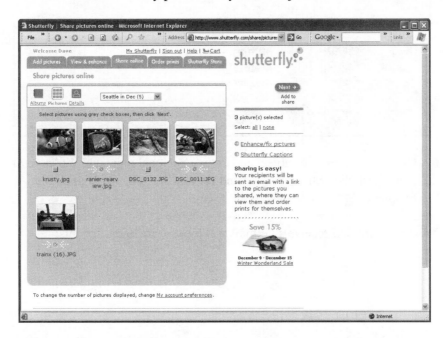

TIP *As you get ready to share your pictures, you can click Enhance/Fix Pictures to improve your images with Shutterfly's free editing tools. You can also add personalized and creative borders to your pictures by clicking the Edit Titles & Descriptions link on the right side of the page. From there, you can enter text and add festive frames to your images.*

4. When you're ready, click Next on the right side of the page.

5. Choose saved e-mail addresses from your Shutterfly address book, or address the message to as many people as you like. Separate each e-mail address with a comma. If you like, you can even upload your address book from Outlook or Palm.

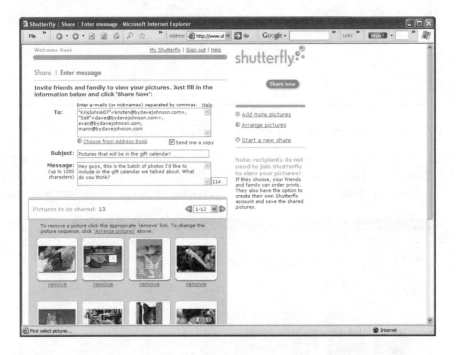

6. Change the message subject and enter a personal message. When you're ready, just click Share now to send the notification e-mail to all the recipients.

Your recipient will receive an e-mail that looks something like this:

The folks who get your e-mail don't have to be Shutterfly members or sign in with a password to see your pictures. They just need to click View album; Shutterfly opens in their web browser, right to the page that displays your pictures.

Your visitors now have several options:

- They can click on individual pictures and view them onscreen.

- They can click View as a Slide Show, which lets them see each picture in the album one after the other as a photo slide show.

- They can click Save Pictures, which will let them order prints of your pictures using Shutterfly's photofinishing service. They can make prints of any or all of your shared pictures in the same way that you can make prints of your own Shutterfly images.

After you share a batch of pictures in Shutterfly, you can always go back and share them again with someone else. They remain in your account for future editing and ordering, so you can reshare them with as many other people as you like, as often as you like.

Sending Images via E-mail

E-mail is another common way to share digital images with people who live far apart. Not only is e-mail good for casually lending images to friends and family, it's also the medium of choice for professionals. E-mail is how some photographers turn in high-resolution images to their editors for publication in newspapers, magazines, and books.

So how do you do it? Sending pictures within e-mail is simply a matter of including one or more images as attachments in your mail message. *Attachments* are sometimes called binary files—as opposed to plain text—that your mail program can deliver to another person's mail system.

Most of the time, attachments work just fine. Occasionally, though, you'll run into problems sending images as attachments. That's because the original Internet wasn't originally designed to accommodate sending big files like pictures via e-mail. Here are some snags you may run into:

- **Beware of sending files that are too big.**   Many e-mail systems can't deal with a single e-mail file that's bigger than about 2MB. For most e-mail transmissions, we'd consider 1MB to be your upper limit on file size, though broadband users (like cable modem and DSL) can often send and receive larger e-mails (up to about 5MB) without trouble. We can't give you a definitive number, though, because it depends upon your Internet provider's rules. If you send a very large file to someone, it can get "stuck" in their mail server, clogging up messages that are trying to come in afterwards. Check the file size of your attachments (see Figure 16-1) before sending them. To ensure that your messages aren't too big, we recommend resizing images that you plan to e-mail down to around 800×600 pixels.

■ **Very old versions of America Online—prior to version 6, for instance— can only receive a single attachment.** Even though most mail systems can accept multiple attached files in each e-mail message, if you know someone who is still using an old edition of AOL, their PC won't know what to make of that kind of message. Only one of the attachments will get to the recipient, and the others will simply disappear into the ether. On the other hand, the newest versions of AOL handle multiple files in a single message just fine—it assembles all the images into a single, convenient ZIP file.

8

| FIGURE 8-1 | This 2.7MB file is, for many folks, simply too large to e-mail effectively. Resize it or change it into another file format (like JPG), so that it's under a megabyte. |

Shrinking Images for E-mail

Having a lot of resolution is a good thing for printing, but 2- and 3-megapixel digital images are cumbersome to send through e-mail. You really should resize pictures in your favorite image editor before attaching them to electronic messages (we explained how to do that back in Chapter 6). In general, e-mail-bound images should be cropped and/or resized down to 600×800 pixels and saved in JPG format. If you remember to do that, you'll never get any complaints from friends or family that your images are too big and are clogging their e-mail system.

If you don't mind spending a few dollars, you can get a specialized program for cropping and resizing images as well. A Smaller Image, from TriVista (www.trivista.com) is a great little program for prepping your photos for e-mail.

This simple $15 program is designed from the ground up to crop and resize photos. After you drag an image into the application window, you can move a cropping frame around the screen until you've composed the picture just the way you want. The cool part is that you can configure the cropping frame's proportion based on how large you want the resulting photo to be, so there's absolutely no guesswork. Set the end photo size to 640×480, for instance, and the cropping frame is proportioned exactly right for the job. You can also scale the cropping frame to include more or less of the original image in the new, resized photo. It's all very clever and makes you wonder why no one has ever thought of that before.

Viewing Images Someone Sent to You

In most e-mail programs (like Netscape Messenger, Microsoft Outlook, or Outlook Express), your attachment appears as an icon that you manipulate like any other file icons. Here are your most common choices:

- With the message window open, right-click and choose the View option to see the image on the desktop without opening a large image editing program.

- Double-click the image icon to launch a preview window or an image editing program and display the image.

- Drag-and-drop the image icon from the message window to the desktop or another Windows folder for permanent storage.

A Smaller Image also includes sharpness, brightness, and contrast controls, an optional graphic border for your images, and a simple text tool for adding captions. If you frequently resize photos for e-mail, the Web, or printing, A Smaller Image is a very handy tool.

Attaching Pictures in E-mail

Though the process varies from one program to another, attaching one or more images to an e-mail message really isn't hard. The basic procedure is this: drag-and-drop an image file directly into your open e-mail message, or use a menu option to insert a file into the message. Almost all mail software uses the paperclip icon as a standard symbol to represent an attachment to your message, so look for that button and use it to specify files for inclusion in your e-mail (see Figure 8-2).

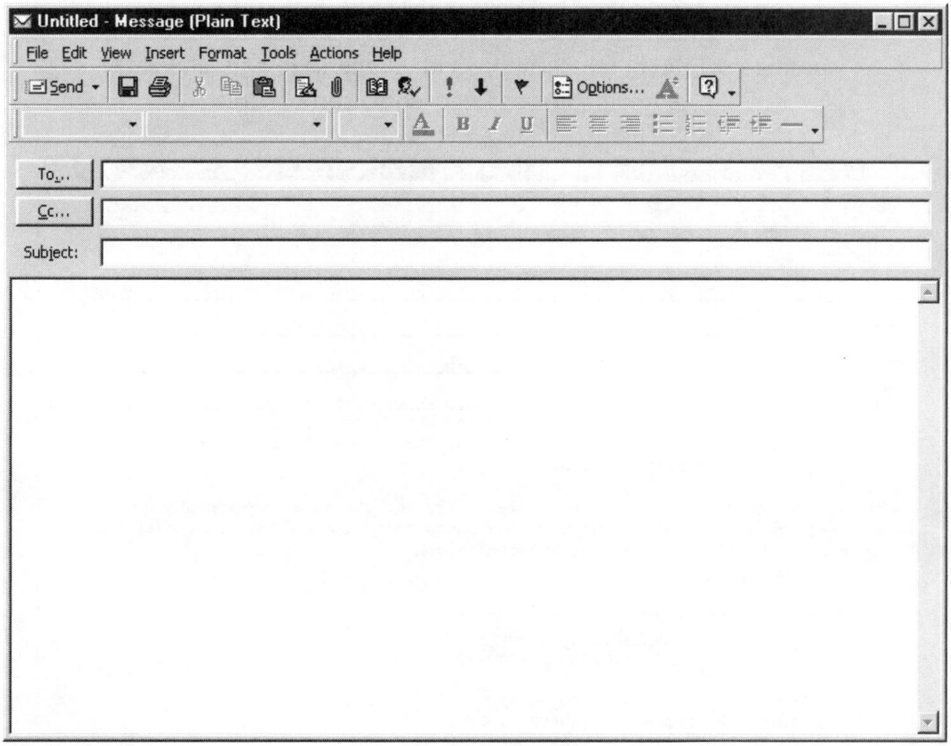

FIGURE 8-2 Use the paperclip icon to attach images (and other kinds of files) to your e-mail.

How to ... Send E-mail with Outlook

If you're a Microsoft Outlook user, here's how to attach a pair of images to an outgoing message:

1. Click the New button in the Outlook toolbar to create a new mail message. A blank, untitled message should appear.

2. Address the e-mail by typing the appropriate e-mail address in the To box.

3. Add a subject by typing in the Subject box, seen in the following illustration.

4. Enter some message text. It's generally a good idea to write a personal, specific note rather than sending a blank message with attachments— that way the recipient knows it's not some sort of virus.

```
We just got a new cat named Molniya! - Message (Plain Text)

File  Edit  View  Insert  Format  Tools  Actions  Help

Send  |  ...

To...     Rick and Shawna Broida

Cc...

Subject:  We just got a new cat named Molniya!

Just like the subject line says, we got a new cat today. She's a 2 year old
Russian Blue and so we're naming her Molniya. The name is kind of appropriate,
actually, since she's pretty eccentric.

(Side note to readers -- I have a special prize for the first person who
understands why an eccentric cat might be named Molniya, and emails me with the
right answer. Email me at dave@bydavejohnson.com.)

Dave
--------------------------------------------
Dave Johnson          www.bydavejohnson.com
                      dave@bydavejohnson.com

Author -  How To Use Digital Video
          Digital Photography Answers
          How To Do Everything With Your Palm Handheld

"I showed this guy my pictures, he said they didn't breathe, I said I painted
them that way" -- Kristin Hersh
```

5. If you have a folder with pictures open on the desktop, you can drag an image file from that folder over the message window and drop it, as shown in the following illustration. You should see an attachment appear in the message.

6. To add another image to the message, choose Insert | File from the message window's menu, or click on the Attachment button (shaped like a paperclip). You should then see the Insert File dialog box.

7. Navigate to the appropriate folder and select the image file you want to attach. If you want to attach multiple files from the same folder, you can hold down the CTRL key while you click on each image file.

8. Click the Insert button to close the Insert File dialog box and insert the images in the message.

9. When your message is complete, click the Send button to send it to its recipient.

Letting Windows Resize Your Pictures

The easiest way to send pictures in e-mail is to let Windows worry about all the resizing stuff. To do that, open the folder that has the pictures you want to send and do this:

1. Select one or more pictures in the folder by clicking with the mouse. Hold down the CTRL key if you want to select more than one picture.

2. Click E-mail the Selected Items from the File and Folder Tasks pane on the right side of the folder. You'll see the Send Pictures via E-mail dialog box appear.

3. Click Make All My Pictures Smaller, and then click OK.

4. Windows will add the selected pictures to a new message window in your usual e-mail program. Address and send the message the way you usually would.

The cool part of this is that the original pictures aren't disturbed, and your recipient gets "shrunk" versions of your pictures with almost no effort on your part!

Sharing Pictures on Disks

Because JPG images are so small, you can often copy a few images to a floppy disk and pass them around that way. After all, nearly everyone has a floppy disk drive, right?

Even better, pretty much everyone can read PC floppy disks—even Mac users. The Macintosh floppy drive can read ordinary PC floppies. That means you can copy a few JPG images to a floppy and give it to a Mac user, and she or he will be able to read the images just fine.

One caveat, though—PCs can't read Macintosh floppies. So Mac users need to be sure the disk is formatted for a PC before doing the handoff. The same is true of Iomega Zip disks, if you happen to use those. A Zip disk made on a Mac cannot be read on a PC. Instead, you'll see an error message saying that the disk isn't formatted.

The New Floppy Disk: CD-R

Floppy disks have some important limitations, though. They don't hold very much data, they're slow, and despite the fact that they've been around forever—or perhaps because of that—they're becoming obsolete. Some new computers come without any floppy drives at all, in fact. The heir to the floppy throne? CD. These days, most new PCs come with CD-RW drives (these are drives that can copy data to blank CD-R and CD-RW discs), If your computer doesn't have a CD-RW drive, you can add one very inexpensively. A CD is a great way to share images, because a CD-R drive is readable by any CD-ROM drive, making it handy for sharing.

To copy pictures to a CD, do this:

1. Insert a blank CD-R disc in your computer's CD-RW drive.

2. Open the folder that contains your pictures, and then select the images you want to copy to CD. Hold down the CTRL key if you want to select more than one picture.

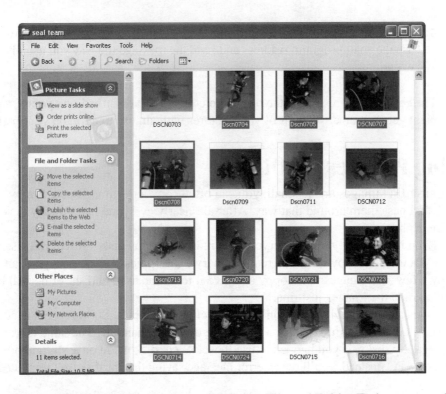

3. Click Copy the Selected Items link in the File and Folder Tasks pane on the left side of the folder. The Copy Items dialog box should appear.

4. In the list of locations, click the entry for your CD-RW drive and click Copy.

5. Next, open My Computer and double-click on the CD-RW drive. Click the link to write the files to the CD, and you'll end up with a disc you can use on any PC to view your pictures.

Strategies for Sharing Lots of Images

If you need to send someone a lot of images and you want to keep the total file size low, you can do a few things:

■ If you use Shutterfly, you can share as many images as you want without an extra compression step or clogging up your recipients' e-mail in-boxes.

■ If sending by e-mail, you don't have to send all 20 pictures in the same message. Break up your collection of images so they span several e-mail messages, with each message weighing in at less than a megabyte or so.

■ Use the compression feature in the JPG format to reduce file size. With many images, you can compress the image significantly before you start to see any obvious degradation due to compression. This is great if you're just passing images around among friends, though we'd be more careful about important pictures that might get printed.

■ Instead of e-mail, mail a CD-R. Because a CD disc holds 650MB of data, you have an awful lot of room to work with. It's certainly more efficient than sending multiple e-mails.

8

Showing off Images on a PDA

People used to show off pictures by carrying them in a purse or wallet. Now you can show off "wallet" pictures the twenty first century way—you can transfer images from your computer to a PDA, handheld computer, or smartphone. If you have a Palm OS PDA like the Zire 71, Tungsten T5, or Sony Clie, or a Pocket PC, it's a snap to turn it into a digital wallet photo collection. A typical PDA can store dozens of images on a memory card and let you display them a picture at a time or in slide show mode.

Applications abound for storing and displaying images on handheld computers. Here are some of the best choices (see Figure 8-3 for a glimpse of what some look like):

■ AcidImage (www.red-mercury.com)

■ SplashPhoto (www.splashdata.com)

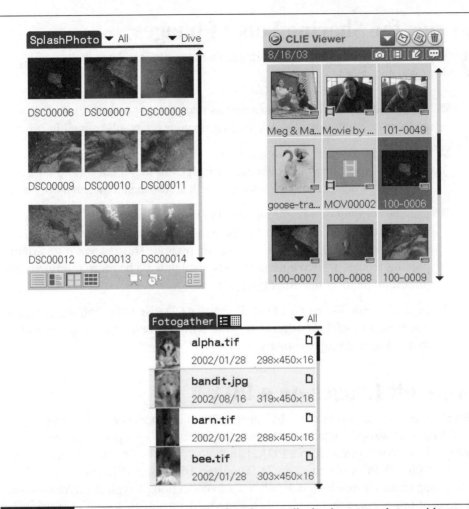

FIGURE 8-3   A variety of photo applications let you display images and even videos on any handheld.

TIP   *Check your device—your PDA may come with its own built-in image viewing software.*

Showing Off Pictures in a Digital Picture Frame

Another way to display digital images is in a digital picture frame. Digital picture frames are inexpensive LCD displays mounted in a picture frame shell. Equipped with a memory card, the picture frame can show digital images in a slide show format. Digital picture frames are readily available. Models include the Ceiva, the Digi-Frame, and Sony's Digital CyberFrame.

Sony's CyberFrame uses Sony's Memory Stick to display both still images and MPEG movies in a small LCD screen that you can place on a tabletop like an ordinary picture frame. If you already have a Sony digital camera that uses Memory Stick memory storage, the CyberFrame is a good choice because you can simply remove the memory card from the camera and insert it directly in the picture frame to begin displaying images. The Digi-Frame is a similar product, though it uses both CompactFlash and SmartMedia memory cards, so you can insert the memory card from most digital cameras to view your images.

The Ceiva, which you can see in Figure 8-4, is unique in two ways: in addition to a small cache of internal (nonremovable) memory, it also connects to the Internet via an ordinary telephone jack. Using a built-in modem, it regularly connects to the Internet and downloads images you've stored on the Ceiva web site. With the ability to rotate among 20 images stored in the Ceiva's memory each day, you can have a constant supply of images on display with minimal effort. Likewise, Ceiva makes it possible to share images from your digital camera with other Ceiva picture frame owners. So you can establish a community of friends and family who exchange images among their picture frames via the Ceiva web site.

8

FIGURE 8-4   Digital picture frames put an always-changing slide show of your digital images right on a table top.

Here is a handy chart showing the digital picture frame makers and their web sites:

Digital Picture Frames	Find It At
Ceiva	www.ceiva.com
Digi-Frame	www.digi-frame.com
Sony CyberFrame	www.sonystyle.com

Showing Pictures on TV

No one likes to admit it, but we all spend the best hours of our lives in the family room within a stone's throw of the television. So while the Web and framed enlargements are two good ways to show off your pictures, nothing beats watching them on the familiar old television. Heck, we can even think of a non-couch-potato reason to show your pictures on a TV: it's the biggest screen in the house, so everyone can see your photos without craning their necks.

Thankfully, showing your digital images on television is frightfully easy. Most digital cameras have video-out ports built right in that can directly display the contents of your camera's memory card on a TV screen. Don't lose the video cable that comes with your camera, though; one end is a standard RCA jack for connecting to the video-in port of a TV or VCR, but the other end is a specialized connector for your camera. Try not to lose this cable—it's not something you can easily replace, because it's only available from the camera manufacturer.

If Your Camera Has No Video Output

Not all digital cameras have video outputs, and if you have one of those video-deprived models, you might still want to show your pictures on the big screen. If that sounds like you, there are still ways to get your photos onto a TV screen.

Many computers, for instance, have their own TV output. Look on the back of your PC. If you see a port, you can connect your computer to a television or VCR. That's called an S-Video connection, and many—perhaps even most—computers sold today have one of these connections. Plug an S-Video cable (which may have come with your computer or is commonly available at any audio/video or computer shop) to your computer and a TV. Switch your TV to its external input, and you should see your PC's display on the TV. From there, it's easy to run a slide show of your images on the PC.

If putting your computer and the TV in the same room doesn't sound like something you want to do, there's yet one more option. You might consider getting a stand-alone "set top" device that displays digital photos on a TV.

Microsoft's TV Photo Viewer, for instance, is a cool little device that looks like an external floppy disk drive. It plugs into your TV's video port and displays pictures from a floppy disk. The gadget comes with Windows software that lets you drag-and-drop images into a custom slide show. You can arrange the images, rotate them, crop pictures, and even add captions. When you're done, the images are copied to a standard floppy in 640×480-pixel resolution, which you can insert into the TV Photo Viewer. If you give one of these guys to your parents, you can make slide shows on floppy disks that you can mail to your folks. They can watch the pictures on their own TV at their leisure.

And Microsoft isn't the only game in town. The SanDisk Digital Photo Viewer (www.sandisk.com) is a similar box that connects to your TV, but it has an array of slots for inserting CompactFlash, SmartMedia, Memory Stick, SD, and MMC cards. The device is designed for no-nonsense simplicity; just insert a memory card from your digital camera and use the bundled remote control to view, zoom, rotate, and step through photos. Or there's the eFilm Picturevision, from Delkin (www.delkin.com). It, too, lets you insert memory cards from digital cameras and display their contents on a TV. Any one of these gadgets can bring back the old-fashioned experience of watching 35mm slides in the living room.

8

Chapter 9

Printing Your Pictures

In this chapter you'll learn to...

■ Order pictures from Shutterfly

■ Decide what size works with your picture's resolution

■ Distinguish among laser, inkjet, and dye sublimation printers

■ Shop for a printer

■ Choose the right kind of paper for your print job

■ Print an enlargement with Paint Shop Pro

■ Configure your printer for paper and quality

■ Determine what side of the paper to print on

■ Care for prints after they come out of the printer

A lot of the time, it all comes down to this: no matter how versatile the digital medium is, a digital camera isn't very useful unless you can get prints of your onscreen bits and bytes. Great prints. Prints that look every bit as good as what you can get from a film camera and the local photo shop.

You're in luck. There's no reason you can't make prints from your digital camera that look just as good as (and possibly even better than) what you used to get from a film camera. You can tweak a digital image so it looks exactly the way you want it to, and you can get prints any way you like—from wallet-sized all the way up to 20×30-inch poster–style.

In this chapter, we'll talk about everything you need to know to get great prints from your digital images, both from Shutterfly and at home on your ink jet printer.

Getting Prints from Shutterfly

There was a time when the only way to get prints from your digital camera was to set up an inkjet printer, pick the right paper and toner, make your own prints and wait while they dry, and resupply the paper and toner when you were finished.

This process can be time-consuming. These days, the smartest and easiest way to get prints is to use an online photo service, like Shutterfly.

After uploading one or more pictures to the Shutterfly web site, you can order excellent quality prints that are processed within 24 hours using traditional photofinishing methods, which will last for generations to come. Shutterfly's chemical process—combined with the use of true Fuji Crystal Archive photo paper—means that your prints will have the same or greater durability as prints from traditional photofinishers.

Shutterfly uses Fujicolor Crystal Archive photographic paper from Fuji. Fuji Crystal Archive paper has long been considered the finest color photographic paper available, and it is the choice of professional photographers and commercial labs. Recent independent studies by Wilhelm Imaging Research show that Crystal Archive is the most fade-resistant photographic paper, outlasting other major brands by almost a three-to-one margin.

Shutterfly uses state-of-the-art equipment that exposes Fuji's Crystal Archive photographic paper using red, green, and blue lasers to produce the sharpest prints available. The exposed photographic paper is chemically processed in the same way as in traditional photo labs. These special printers, combined with Shutterfly's proprietary imaging technology, result in the best possible prints from your pictures.

Once developed, your photographs are either mailed to you or directly to friends and family within just a couple of days. Shutterfly has all the advantages of old-fashioned film processing, but saves you a trip to the store. Plus, you have the added advantage of being able to select only the prints you want, and you can crop the pictures before you print them. You can also remove red eye, and you can even add captions and other flourishes.

Getting Started

As you probably know, *resolution* refers to the number of pixels in an image. Resolution is sometimes referred to by the width and height of the image, as well as the total number of pixels in the image. For example, an image that is 1200 pixels high and 1600 pixels wide (1200×1600) contains 1,920,000 pixels (or about 2 megapixels).

When you order a picture from Shutterfly, you may get a "not recommended" message. This means that the resolution of your picture is too low for the size of print you want. You should compare the resolution of your picture with resolution guidelines in this chart to help you print the best pictures possible:

Image Resolution	Maximum print size
Less than 640×480	Only wallet-size prints
1024×768	4×6
1152×864	5×7
1600×1200	8×10

For large-format prints (like 11×14, 16×20, and 20×30), Shutterfly's recommendations are similar to those for an 8×10, although you'll get better results with pictures that are 3 megapixels or larger.

Can you check the resolution of your pictures from Shutterfly itself? Absolutely. Go to the View page and click on the thumbnail image; you will then see a larger version of the picture, with recommended print sizes. Above these, hold your cursor over the lowercase *i*. There, you will find the resolution, along with other information.

In addition to analyzing the resolution of each image within your collection, Shutterfly also analyzes each image, and then automatically applies adjustments (called VividPics) to the picture to improve the exposure and colors.

However, if you have already edited your pictures for color, brightness, or contrast in an application such as Paint Shop Pro or Adobe Photoshop, we recommend that you turn off the VividPics setting for the edited pictures. To do this, select the desired picture and click Enhance on the green navigation bar. Then click the Effects tab. On the bottom right, click the check box that turns off the VividPics setting for that picture. If you have a number of pictures selected, you can use the link to the left of your picture to apply this effect to all selected pictures. Pictures printed with this setting turned off will be printed exactly as they were uploaded, with no automatic image adjustments or corrections.

Ordering Prints

Ordering prints at Shutterfly is pretty simple. Just follow these steps:

1. Choose the Shutterfly album that contains the pictures you want to order. This can be done by clicking on the album itself or on the check box below the album.

2. Or, if the pictures you want to print aren't already stored on Shutterfly, begin by adding them. Click the Add Pictures tab at the top of the page. Choose whether to add the pictures to an existing album already on Shutterfly or to create a new one. Then click Next.

It's time to add the pictures to Shutterfly from your computer. You can either drag file icons from Windows directly onto the drag-and-drop area of the web page or click Choose pictures and pick them from the dialog. After you select some pictures, they'll upload automatically. Bigger image files will take longer to complete. When they're done, click View pictures.

3. Click a picture in your album and you'll see it appear in the View & Enhance tab. Take note of the Prints Best Up To information under the picture: it suggests a maximum print size based on the resolution of the image.

4. If you want to make any changes to the picture before it prints, now is the time. Refer to Chapters 6 and 7 for details on how to remove red eye, crop, and otherwise modify your picture using the tools built right into Shutterfly.

5. Click Order Prints. On the next page, you can select how many and what size to print. The default quantity and size in each order is one 4×6 print. Also located at the top of this page is an option to select which type of paper finish you would like: matte or glossy. By default, the filename of each picture will be printed on the back of each print. You can, instead, choose to type in your own custom text up to 80 characters (for example, "Molly's first bite of pizza!"). When the order is set up the way you want it, click Next.

9

TIP *If you are planning to make three copies of a single picture and you want to send one of each to three different people, only specify one print on this page. When you select the recipients on the next page, each will get one print. If you select two prints on this page, each recipient will get two copies.*

6. Select the recipients for your prints. It's easy to send prints to as many people as you want. On the Select Recipients page, simply check the boxes next to the names of the people you want to send prints to. You can customize each recipient's order on the next page. To add someone new to the list, click the Add New Address button.

7. Once you finish selecting recipients and have reviewed your order, click the Next button to Select Payment Options. Shutterfly accepts payment by personal checks, money orders, or cashier's checks denominated in U.S. dollars. Review your billing info (and edit it, if necessary), enter a gift certificate code if you have one, and then choose a payment method (credit card or check) and click Place My Order Now.

A confirmation and thank you appears, letting you know your order has been placed. An order number and further instructions are provided (for instance, instructions on how to cancel your order within the first hour of placing it, or

The Difference Between Professional and Home Printing

So, you can make your own prints from home or order prints from professional photofinishers like Shutterfly. Which is better? Which should you do? For the most part, it all comes down to the actual printing method.

Professional photofinishers use a process called continuous tone printing, while inkjet printers at home use halftone printing. *Continuous tone printing* gets its name from the fact that the pigments used to make the picture work like the grains on film—they can exhibit gradual color change without any abrupt transitions because the professional printer can generate any desired color for each dot. It's the best and most realistic way to print a picture.

Inkjet printers can't create continuous tones; instead, they lay down dots of distinct color. And, as you may remember from school, when you place two colors right next to each other and step back, the human eye perceives a third color, rather than the primary colors. That's the essence of *halftone printing* at home: lots of little color dots creating a rainbow effect.

While halftone printing can look great—just check out the sample prints in the printer section of an electronics store to see for yourself—professional prints will look better because continuous tone printing can generate sharper images from the same number of pixels.

instructions on sending a check for payment). You may want to print this page to have a record of your confirmation number. (You will also receive an e-mail containing this confirmation number.) Your prints will arrive in a few days.

Ordering Several Shutterfly Prints

That's the process for printing a single picture. But what if you have an entire album you'd like to print? Do you have to print the images one at a time? Nope— you can select several at once.

To do that, go to the View & Enhance tab and open an album. With the pictures in the album displayed on the web page, click the check box for every picture that you intend to print, and then click Order Prints. If you want to print the entire album, you can skip the check boxes and click Order Prints. Shutterfly will send the entire album to its state-of-the-art photofinishing lab for you.

On the next page, you can specify the print sizes, quantities, and type of finish (matte or glossy) just like you did when printing a single picture. Want to adjust cropping? Not a problem. Just click the thumbnail of a picture and you'll get the same crop options that you first saw in Chapter 6.

9

Printing at Home: Picking the Right Print Size

The traditional world of film photography made printing enlargements easy, because you didn't have to think much about factors like resolution. Everyone knows that you can take a roll of film to the corner store and make pretty much any size prints you like, from wallet-size to 8×10. That's because all film cameras start with the same size originals. Digital cameras are not all the same, though, so you need to consider the resolution of a picture—how many pixels it has—when you decide on a print size.

As a general rule, most printers lay down between 150 and 200 dots per inch (dpi) as they make a print. That means, on a 200-dpi printer, a digital picture that measured 200×200 pixels would measure an inch across when printed. So, when we talk about the ideal print size for digital photos, all we do is divide the number of pixels in the picture by the printer's resolution, such as 150 or 200. That tells us how big you can safely print the picture. Or, put another way, you can take a standard print size, such as 8×10 inches, and multiply it by the printer resolution to find out how many pixels should be in the image for ideal printing.

Of course, that begs the question: what is your printer's resolution? What number should you use? Well, here's where it gets interesting. Printers vary, but, in general, you can assume that the typical resolution for an inkjet printer is 150–300 dots per inch.

So, armed with that knowledge, here's a chart you can use to predict if your picture will print well at home:

Print Size (inches)	Good Results	Best Results
4×6	768×1024 (less than 1 megapixel)	800×1200 (1 megapixel)
5×7	864×1152 (1 megapixel)	1000×1400 (just over 1 megapixel)
8×10	1200×1600 (2 megapixels)	1600×2000 (3 megapixels)
11×14	1600×2100 (3 megapixels)	2200×2800 (6 megapixels)
16×20	1600×2100 (3 megapixels)	2200×2800 (6 megapixels)
20×30	1600×2100 (3 megapixels)	2400×3400 (8 megapixels)

What happens if you don't have enough pixels for a given print size? Does the printer break? Does the print come out blank? No, of course not. But let's consider an extreme example: suppose you tried printing a tiny digital picture that measured just 200×200 pixels as an 8×10-inch print. The print would have just 25 dots per inch, and that would look terrible, like a highly magnified newspaper photograph in which you'd see the dots (as in Figure 9-1). The photo would be a blurry mess.

FIGURE 9-1   What a very small digital photo would look like printed at 8×10 inches.

That means if you're a little short on pixels, you might be able to get away with printing it at slightly more than the ideal size for the image. But if you go too far and try to make a print that's too big, the image might look terrible.

Are you surprised by the bottom of the table? It takes a lot of pixels to make high-quality prints. But does it really mean that you need an 8-megapixel camera to make a 20×30-inch print?

Yes and no. Many printers will give you great results even if you feed them an image that's somewhat underpixeled. In other words, suppose you have a 1600×1200-pixel image. You can still get quite decent results by printing it at 16×20 inches or perhaps even 20×30. We've certainly gotten good results that way.

Printing on Your Own

If you ask us, the easiest way to print digital photos is to click a few times on the Shutterfly web site and be done with it. But we know that's not the only way people ever print: there are times when you've got to make a print instantly, be it for a last minute gift or a school project. Real life demands immediate prints occasionally, and that's exactly what digital photography can deliver. Of course, that also means buying your own photo printer.

9

Choosing a Printer

Let's talk about how to choose the right printer for your needs. Buying a printer isn't always an easy decision because not only are there many different brands of printers competing for your attention—and lots of different models from each manufacturer—but you also have to figure out what kind of printer you want. If you're serious about printing your own digital images, you'll probably want an inkjet printer. But, to be sure, let's talk about the variety of printers you can choose from.

Laser Printers

A *laser printer* is like a specialized photocopier. Using the digital image in the computer's memory as a template, a laser printer electrically charges each piece of paper. The printer then allows *toner*—a fine ink-like powder—to come into contact with the paper. (See Figure 9-2 for a look at a typical toner cartridge.) The toner sticks to the paper in places where it has an electrostatic charge, and the toner is finally permanently melted into the paper by a very hot fusing wire.

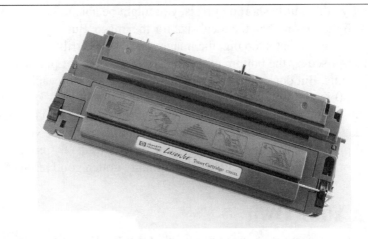

FIGURE 9-2   A laser printer's toner cartridge is generally good for several thousand black-and-white prints.

Laser printers have some advantages. They can print quickly (many personal laser printers can generate as many as eight or ten pages per minute), and the toner lasts a long time, yielding a very low cost per page. A common laser printer like the HP LaserJet 1200 prints about 3,000 to 5,000 sheets of paper for each $80 toner cartridge. Those advantages add up to a good all-around office printer that handles most common print jobs pretty well. Personal laser printers can be had for between $100 and $500, with many excellent models priced under $300.

Unfortunately, laser printers tend to be better at printing text than graphics. That's mainly because most laser printers are black-and-white devices, able to generate just shades of gray. Color laser printers are available, but because they're priced at $750 and up, they're pretty expensive. Even if you could purchase a color laser printer, we wouldn't recommend it for printing digital images. Color laser printers tend to produce output that doesn't look much like traditional photo prints and, thus, it doesn't look good framed. They also limit you to a print size of 8×10 inches.

Laser printers can certainly be used to print images, and they can do it well, as long as your needs don't include color. You can print a large quantity of family newsletters with a laser printer faster than with an inkjet, for instance.

Inkjet Printers

If you want to print images, inkjet printers are the best all-around printing solution for most people. They produce excellent color output, but they can also print text at a reasonable speed—as long as you don't need to print a lot of it.

Inkjet printers are, in some ways, a simpler technology than laser printers. Simply put, *inkjet printers* work by spraying microscopic droplets of ink onto paper. You can see an inkjet's internals—complete with ink cartridges—in Figure 9-3. Of course, it gets a lot more complicated than that. Printer manufacturers exert a lot of effort making sure the dots are small; that they combine with other dots to mimic thousands of distinct colors; that they dry fast enough so they don't spread, run, or smear; and that the paper is optimized to handle the ink's chemical characteristics. It's a very technical business.

Nonetheless, we generally don't have to worry about most of that stuff. What matters is inkjet printers create good output and they're pretty affordable, typically running between $50 and $500.

We sometimes run into people who are concerned about inkjet quality based on experiences they had with older printers. But those fears are relatively unfounded today. Inkjet technology has dramatically improved over the years.

Dye Sublimation Printers

The smallest segment of the printer market is occupied by dye sublimation printers (also called dye-subs for short). Look inside a dye-sublimation printer, and you'll see a long roll of transparent film that appears to be sheets of red-, blue-, yellow-,

9

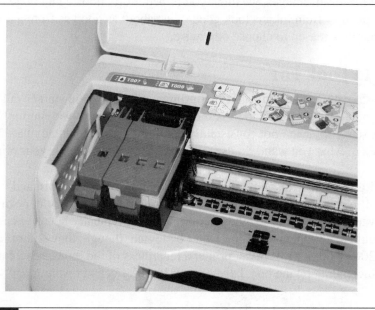

FIGURE 9-3   The print head slides back and forth across the page, spraying dots of ink as it goes.

and gray-colored cellophane. The film is composed of solid dyes corresponding to the four basic colors used in printing: cyan, magenta, yellow, and black (CMYK). The print head heats as it passes over the film, causing the dyes to vaporize and permeate the glossy surface of the paper before they return to solid form. Because the dye gets absorbed and goes just below the surface of the paper, the process is called *dye-sublimation*. Because the color infuses the paper, it is also less vulnerable to fading and distortion over time. Dye-sub printers also create "continuous tone" images—there are no dots whatsoever, something you tend to get with inkjet printers. Bottom line: the results from dye-sub printers are great.

The downside is dye-sub printers are not much good for printing text, so your dye-sub printer will have to be a second printer, which you only use when you're expressly printing photos. For us, a bigger disadvantage is that dye-sub printers typically only create 5×7-inch or perhaps 8×10-inch prints—nothing larger. Also, the selection of printer models is much more limited and much more expensive. You can find some printers in the $300–500 range, but full-page, 8×10-inch prints require bigger printers that tend to start at $1,000. These printers are more commonly used in the professional arena, where publishers can inexpensively make test prints that show what output from the final printing press will eventually look like.

Make no mistake: output from dye sublimation printers looks wonderful. But, given all the disadvantages, we think you're better off choosing an inkjet. And, because pictures from inkjets look good—just about as good as from a dye-sub— there's hardly a reason to choose otherwise.

What to Look For

So let's say you want to buy an inkjet printer. Where do you start? Walk into a store and all printers tend to look more or less the same. And, in our humble opinion, salespeople are not consistently helpful unless you already have a pretty good idea of what you want. So use this checklist to help choose your printer:

■ **Resolution**   Resolution is measured in dots per inch (dpi), and virtually all laser printers print at 600 or 1200dpi. In the inkjet world, resolution varies quite a bit, though better printers will typically be advertised as either 2880dpi or 1440dpi. Don't be fooled, though, they still print around 200–300dpi. Most inkjet printers, regardless of the thousands-of-dots-per-inch rating on the box, have a much lower effective resolution.

- **Number of inks**   This is irrelevant for a laser printer, of course, but when you're inkjet shopping, look for a printer that uses a pure black cartridge instead of mixing all the other colors to mimic black. (The result is a muddy gray-brown instead of black, and these printers use up their ink exceptionally fast.) Better inkjet printers use five or more independent ink color cartridges to create more realistic photo prints, but four cartridges (black plus three colors) is the absolute minimum you should accept. You can also save money on replacement inks by buying a printer that has separate cartridges for each color. That way, when one color runs low, you don't have to replace all the inks at once.

- **Speed**   You should pay attention to the printer's speed (measured in pages per minute, or ppm) and resolution. Slow laser printers run at 8ppm; the fastest run around 24ppm. Remember that inkjets print much more slowly; color is their selling point, not speed.

- **Eyeball the prints**   No matter what the specs say, a printer is only as good as the prints. Try out printers in the store before you buy. Most computer stores have demo models set up that spit out prints when you press a test button. And, as we mention in the section "Working with Printer Paper," remember that the paper is just as important to print quality as the ink and printer itself.

- **Connectivity**   Once you get the basic specs down, you might want to consider ease of use. If you have a notebook PC or a handheld computer, you might want a printer that includes an infrared or Bluetooth port for wireless printing. And, if you have a network at home, you might want a printer with built-in Ethernet, so you can connect the printer directly to your network.

- **Direct printing**   Some printers let you connect your digital camera directly to the printer or insert the camera's memory card into the printer. This lets you circumvent the PC for fast and painless printing.

- **Size and capacity**   Although most major manufacturers like Epson, Canon, and HP all make good printers that generate excellent results, they differ dramatically in terms of what kind of paper they can print on. Most printers print up to 8.5×11-inches. You'll have to buy a wide-format printer if you want to create 11×17- or 13×19-inch prints.

The Real Resolution of an Inkjet

Confused? We said earlier that inkjet printers come in resolutions up to 2880dpi, yet now we claim that they print at 150 or 200dpi. Which is it? How can one number be so different from the other?

It is confusing. The simplest answer is that printer companies can be misleading. The resolution they advertise on the box isn't a measure of how many pixels per inch (ppi) the printer can accurately lay down on paper. If it were, 2880dpi ink jets would be capable of printing photos around professional magazine quality, and that's not the case. So something else must be going on.

Indeed. Here's the deal: the advertised resolution of an inkjet printer is a measure of the accuracy of mechanical systems like the step motor that drives the print head around on the page and the precision of the nozzles themselves. Certainly, you want the printer to be as accurate as possible, but keep in mind that it takes several steps for the print head to make even a single dot on the paper—and, in the end, it's the dots that limit the printer's maximum resolution. So, an ink jet with a resolution of 2880dpi is not necessarily a whole lot better than an ink jet with a resolution of 1440dpi. Visually, prints made with one printer may look a bit better than the other, but certainly not twice as good. It's like buying a 3 GHz computer. It's faster than a 1.5 GHz PC, but it's not twice as fast.

Put another way, a printer with a lousy step motor can visibly degrade the quality of a print, but buying a printer that has a 10,000dpi resolution will only result in more perfectly formed pixels. But the pixels themselves will be limited by other factors.

The printer's top resolution is, indeed, important, but other factors play an important role as well: using the sharpening filter on your image and choosing the right paper can have just as much of an effect on the final print quality.

So what resolution should you use when you print? The honest-to-goodness dpi of most ink jet printers is still in the range of 150–300dpi. If you start with a sharp image and plan to use high-quality inkjet paper, you might see a small difference in image quality if you feed the printer a 300dpi image. But the difference will be small, and you can generally get decent results with as little as 200dpi. If you send images of lower resolution to the printer, you'll be able to tell the difference.

■ **Dye versus pigment**   If you're shopping for an inkjet printer, you should know that most models use dye-based inks, while higher-end designs sometimes rely on pigment-based inks. If you're concerned about generating prints that are highly resistant to fading, investigate pigment-based printers. On average, you'll find that run-of-the-mill (dye-based) inkjets can make fade-resistant prints last for 10–20 years. Pigment-based printers generate prints that should last for 75–100 years. On the other hand, cheaper dye-based inks are brighter and more vivid than more expensive (but longer life) pigment-based inks.

Some image editors and print programs use DPI (dots per inch) instead of—or in addition to—pixels. And we've found that a lot of people are mystified when it comes to understanding the relationship between resolution, dpi, print size, and pixels. What, really, is a dialog box telling you when it says that an image is 4×6 inches, 72dpi?

The important thing to understand is that measurements like 4×6 inches and 72dpi are meaningless while the image is still on a PC. A computer deals only in pixels. An image can be 640×480, 1280×1024, or 2240×1680 pixels, for instance. And the size of the image on a computer screen depends upon two things: the screen size of the Windows desktop and the zoom factor of the application displaying the image. If you show a 640×480-pixel image on a Windows desktop that's only 640×480 itself, the image takes up the whole screen. If you show it on a PC that's using a 1280×1024 pixel screen, then the image will be tiny, taking up just part of the screen. The bottom line: when it's still in the virtual world of a computer, the only image size that has any real meaning is the number of pixels used to create it.

Only when you're getting ready to print a picture does a size like 4×6 inches have any meaning. If you assume that there's a one-for-one relationship between a pixel and a printed dot, then the size the image prints at is determined by dividing the number of pixels in the image by the dpi rating you hope to print with.

Consider the same 2240×1680 pixel image. It can make a:

■ **7.5×5.5-inch print** when set to 300dpi (an ideal setting for a color laser printer, for instance)

■ **15×11-inch print** at 150dpi (a resolution that works well on an inkjet printer)

■ **31×23-inch print** when set to 72dpi (on a computer screen)

9

dpi and print size is just one way to measure how large you can print a digital image. The numbers that really tell you the true size of the image are the number of pixels.

Working with Printer Paper

Here's a common scenario: you see great, photorealistic prints in a computer store and think, "That's the printer for me. It's only $150 and it makes outstanding pictures!" So you buy the printer and bring it home. But when you get the printer set up and send your first few images to it, you're devastated. The output is horrible. The prints don't feel like real photographs. They look flat and lifeless. The paper curls. What went wrong?

It's the paper. What you failed to consider is that the choice of paper is so important to the quality of your prints that it's essentially *more important than the printer itself!* A handful of printers on the market can generate photorealistic prints. But, unless you use quality paper, they will all disappoint you.

Which Paper Is Best

Unfortunately, choosing paper isn't easy, even if you know you want to get the best. There are a lot of choices, and it isn't generally clear which kind is best, based on the name or description on the package. This is especially true for inkjet printers. We honestly don't know why paper manufacturers make this so hard; it seems counterproductive to sales.

As a general rule, you'll find store shelves stocked with paper divided into four quality levels: inkjet paper, high-quality inkjet paper, photo quality paper, and glossy photo paper.

So where do you start? Let's begin with daily use that doesn't involve printing photos—you should use either plain paper or inkjet paper. Even when printing on plain paper, use quality stock, because cheap paper can plug the nozzles and decrease the effective resolution of the printer. Of course, we assume that the majority of what you print is just test prints, text, and other routine output. If every print you make is destined for The Louvre, then you might want to skip directly to the section where we talk about photo paper.

When you're ready to step up to some higher-quality printing, you have a number of choices on store shelves (see Figure 9-4). Here's a general overview of the various grades available:

- **Plain paper**   This is good for general text and ordinary graphics printing. The paper is inexpensive, but the ink tends to absorb quickly into the paper and blur the image. The paper also curls and distorts.

■ **Inkjet paper (and high-quality inkjet paper)**   This is a step up and embeds clay or some other ink fixture into the paper to stop the inks from spreading before they dry. For most printing, you won't notice a big difference, but this paper makes for better draft-quality photographic prints.

■ **Photo paper**   A variation of coated paper, photo paper is generally bright-white coated paper that's designed explicitly for photographs. If you're looking for paper in an intermediate price range that can give decent results, try this.

■ **Glossy photo paper**   The best paper around, this stuff is expensive, generally costing about a dollar a sheet. Certainly you won't use it all the time, but if you plan to frame a picture or give your digital prints away to family or friends, definitely use the special photo paper. Note that you can only print on one side of photo paper; the back side looks like the back of a photograph and generally has a logo printed there. We don't recommend printing on the back of glossy paper, even on a laser printer.

9

FIGURE 9-4   With so many choices on store shelves, it pays to experiment with a few different kinds to find the paper that delivers the best output with your printer.

Other Specialty Papers

In addition to ordinary plain, coated, and photo paper, printer manufacturers and paper vendors sell a variety of other specialty papers. You might want to investigate these papers, because they can be a lot of fun and enable you to do all sorts of things with your printer that you never imagined possible:

■ **Greeting card paper**   Greeting card paper and matching envelopes let you make your own greeting cards with your printer and some greeting card software.

■ **Transparency paper**   This clear film media is perfect for printing color overhead slides for business meetings. You can use this to print PowerPoint slides or any other kind of image or document.

■ **T-shirt transfer paper**   This special paper is really an iron-on transfer that you can run through your printer, and then apply to clothing. When you print on T-shirt paper, be sure to use special T-shirt transfer software or just reverse your image before you print. (Create a mirror image of what you want it to look like.)

■ **Fabric sheets**   This unique kind of printing media is fabric that gives your prints texture. You can print on it just for its own sake or use the print to make cross-stitch designs and other craft projects.

9

Which Brand?

What brand of paper should you use? Should you use Epson in an Epson printer and Canon paper in a Canon printer, or should you buy paper from a company like Ilford—known in 35mm photography circles for its excellent paper—instead? This is a good question. Obviously, each printer company wants you to use its own brand of paper with its printer.

In truth, vendors like Canon, Epson, and HP go to great lengths to fine-tune their paper to match their inks, so colors won't bleed and they'll be as vivid as possible. Take our experience with the Epson Stylus Photo 1270, for instance: it does best with Epson's Premium Glossy Photo paper. We tried a dozen different kinds of papers, including paper from companies like Ilford and Tetenal, which came highly recommended by computer and photography store salespeople. After being disappointed with all of those other brands, we tried Epson's own Premium Glossy paper, and were impressed—the results were dramatically better.

How to ...   **Make a Print in Paint Shop Pro**

Now that you have all the parts in place, it's time to print. We'll show you how to make a print of a specific size in Paint Shop Pro; other programs use a similar method. Of course, if printing the picture at a very specific size (like 5×7 or 8×10) isn't important to you, just click the Print button and get it over with. But if you want to print your image so it fits properly in a traditional picture frame, here's how. Specifically, let's say we're going to make a print at 8×10 inches. Do this:

1. Load the paper in your printer. Make sure that you put it in with the appropriate side set for printing, and only load a single sheet at a time.

2. Load the picture you want to print in Paint Shop Pro. The first thing you want to do is crop it to print at the right proportion. Click the Crop tool and drag it through the image, creating a rough crop of your image. At this point, it's not important to be accurate; just make a crop box.

3. In the Tool Options toolbar atop the screen, set the Units to Inches, and then enter the dimensions of your print—width of **8** and height of **10**. Click the check box for Maintain Aspect Ratio.

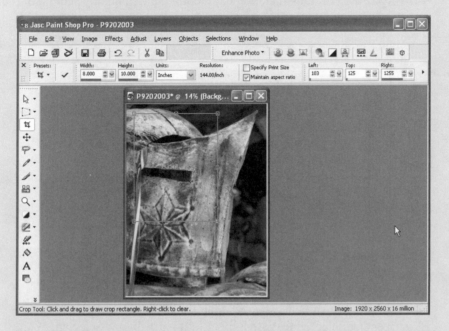

4. Now position the crop box precisely on the screen and resize it by dragging one of the corners. Because the aspect ratio is locked, it'll keep the proper proportions for your 8×10-inch print. When you're happy with the final result, click the check box to make the crop, and you'll get an image that's proportioned exactly right for an 8×10-inch print:

5. Now we're going to select the paper size and orientation. Choose File | Print from the main menu. You should see the Print dialog box.

6. Click the Portrait or Landscape button in the Orientation section of the dialog box to get the image oriented properly.

7. Click the Printer button to open your printer's preferences, and find the paper size selector. Choose 8.5×11, if it isn't already selected. While you're there, select the appropriate type of paper, such as inkjet paper or photo glossy. Click OK to close the printer dialog box.

> **CAUTION** *If you don't tell the print driver about the kind of paper you're printing with, the results will invariably be disappointing.*

8. If you click Fit to Page, the image is printed using all the available page space. Instead, click Center on Page.

9. Now specify the width of the image as 8 inches. You should see the height adjust automatically to 10 inches.

10. Click the Print button to start the print process.

11. When the paper comes out of the printer, leave it there to dry for several minutes. Don't handle it until you're sure it's dry; otherwise, you could smudge it.

So what should you do? If you have a few dollars to spare, buy a bunch of different paper packages and try them out. Print the same image on different kinds of paper and lay them out, side-by-side, in good light. Determine which one is best, and stick with that brand of paper.

Which Side Is the Right Side?

Often, it matters which side of the page you print on. Plain-old laser paper is the same on both sides, so if you print on a laser printer or you use plain paper in an inkjet, it doesn't matter. But if you print on specialty paper in an inkjet printer, make sure you load the paper the right way. Keep these tips in mind:

- Usually, the brighter or shinier side of the paper is the printing side. Occasionally, it's rough, like sandpaper.

- If you're printing on photo paper, the back will probably have a company logo on it.

- Many paper types label the paper with small marks to indicate the proper print side.

Be sure you look carefully at the print directions the first time you try a new paper. Ink won't adhere well—or at all—to the wrong side of specialty papers, and you could end up with a real mess in and around your printer if the ink runs everywhere.

Can you print on both sides of the paper? We get that question a lot. And the answer is that it depends. Don't ever try to print on the back of glossy premium paper, but you can usually print on both sides of inkjet and high-quality inkjet paper without any trouble. If you are printing a newsletter or greeting card, you might print the pictures on one side and use a laser printer to add text to the back.

Caring for Your Prints

All pictures, no matter how they were printed or where they came from, tend to fade over time. Inkjet photos, though, tend to fade somewhat faster. In fact, inkjet inks are sensitive to ultraviolet light, and your images will fade faster if exposed to direct sunlight for extended periods. If you plan to frame pictures and leave them exposed to sunlight, consider using UV-shielded glass, available at some framing shops.

TIP

Keep your original image files on your hard disk or archived on CD-ROM, so you can reprint them when the fading becomes noticeable. Don't delete your pictures just because you printed them.

Some newer printers are marketed specifically as models that create prints with more lightfastness than older printers. You can probably guess that *lightfastness* is a print's capability to resist fading when exposed to light. In addition, you can find some inkjet printers designed to offer extremely long resistance to fading. Intended for serious photo enthusiasts and professionals, pigment-based inkjet printers, like the Epson Stylus Photo 2200, are a bit more expensive than dye-based inkjets, but they can deliver a print life of over 100 years. By comparison, 35mm prints tend to be lightfast for only about 50 years, so newer printers can create prints that last longer than traditional prints.

No matter what kind of printer, ink, or paper you use, you should protect your prints from fading from the moment you print them. Here are a few precautions you can take:

- Cover the print with glass or plastic as soon as it's completely dry (wait 12–24 hours after the print is complete). Contaminants in the air can fade a print quickly, but if you put it under glass or in a photo album, the print is no longer in direct contact with air and, thus, is protected. Some ink and paper combinations can cause a print to fade dramatically in a matter of days if left exposed to the open air.

- Keep the print out of direct sunlight, even when under glass. Hang the print where the sun doesn't shine directly on the wall.

- Avoid handling the print in such a way that you touch the ink with your fingers.

9

Chapter 10

Projects for Parents and Kids

In this chapter you'll learn to...

- Turn images into wallpaper for the Windows desktop

- Show your pictures using the Windows screen saver

- Create your own greeting cards

- Make wrapping paper and book covers

- Add pictures to letterhead in Word

- Stage a Mystery Photo Contest

- Design greeting cards on the PC

- Turn pictures into jigsaw puzzles

- Make a Photo Journal

- Create a photo collage

- Make a family or holiday newsletter

- Create a custom calendar

- Put your family on a magazine cover

- Shake hands with Elvis

- Put your kids in a jar

Over the course of this book, you've learned how to use your digital camera, transfer pictures to the computer, and then touch up and print the ones you like. That's great; consider yourself an official graduate of the Shutterfly Digital Camera School. So isn't it time you and your kids had some fun with your digital photos?

That's where this chapter comes in. In this final chapter, we'll introduce you to some cool projects you can do with your photos. Some of these are things your kids can probably do on their own—like creating Windows wallpaper or making their own personalized wrapping paper. Some are projects you may have to lend a hand with—like making greeting cards, family newsletters, and goofy images you can print and share.

Using Digital Images as Wallpaper

Let's start with something that's not only easy, but also can make your PC a lot more fun. Your Windows desktop can display any kind of image as long as it's been saved in JPG, GIF, or BMP format. If your desktop still has that same old blue or green background—or, heavens forbid, a picture of the computer company's logo—you can use an image from your digital camera to brighten things. To display your picture on your desktop, do this:

1. Make sure your image is in the right format. As you know by now, most digital cameras save images in JPG format, so you're probably ready to go. Windows can't display a TIF or RAW image on the desktop, though.

2. Right-click the desktop and choose Properties from the context menu. The Display Properties dialog box appears.

3. On the Desktop tab, click the Browse button to choose the image.

4. If you want the image centered in your display, choose Center in the Display drop-down menu. If you'd prefer the image to repeat itself all across the display, choose Tile instead. If the image is smaller than the screen, Stretch will make it go from edge-to-edge, but it might distort the picture.

5. Click OK to close the dialog box.

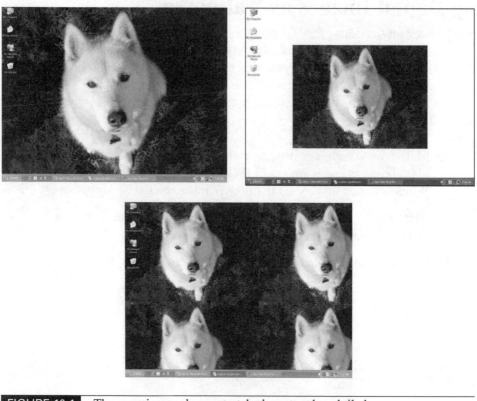

FIGURE 10-1   The same image shown stretched, centered, and tiled

We think centering looks good—tiling photographs just looks busy and can be a bit annoying (see Figure 10-1). Of course, you can experiment and arrange your display any way you like. And if the various members of your family all have their own separate login for the computer, everyone can select their own wallpaper, and the appropriate one will start when each person logs into the PC.

Turn Your Pictures into Screen Savers

The same is true of the Windows screen saver—everyone in the family can select their own, and it'll start displaying after a certain period of inactivity. These days, most monitors don't need screen savers to protect them from old-time dreaded "burn in," but screen savers are still fun to watch, which is why so many people use them.

Windows XP has a screen saver that works by showing off your digital photos. To use it, do this:

1. Right-click on the Windows desktop and choose Properties.

2. On the Display Properties dialog box, click the Screen Saver tab.

3. From the Screen saver list, choose My Pictures Sideshow. Now, you can click OK and Windows will use some smart default settings to show the pictures on your hard disk whenever you stop using the computer for some short period of time. But you can customize the settings by continuing on to the next step.

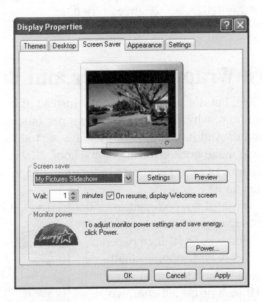

4. Click the Settings button to see the Options page. Here, you can specify how frequently the pictures change, how much of the screen they should take up, and if Windows should use transitions between the pictures. Most importantly, you can tell Windows exactly where to find your photos—handy if you keep them somewhere other than the My Pictures folder, or if you only want to show certain images.

5. When you're happy with the screen saver, click OK twice.

10

Do it in Shutterfly: Cool Projects

In this chapter, we talk a lot about things you can do with your digital photos—projects like greeting cards and photo journals, to name a few.

Don't forget that Shutterfly can professionally print all sorts of cool projects and photo gifts. To start, visit Shutterfly (www.shutterfly.com), log in, and click the Shutterfly Store tab at the top of the screen.

From there, you can order prints and specialty gifts, create cards, and design custom coffee-table books called Photo Books. There are also Snapbooks—spiral-bound mini photo albums that you might order to showcase your child's best photo journal, for instance. Or, collect a dozen of your favorite pet pictures and turn them into a full-size, personalized Calendar.

Make Your Own Wrapping Paper and Book Covers

Wrapping paper is fine, but it's rather impersonal. Instead of buying plain blue wrapping paper with stars, why not create your own personalized paper littered with your own pictures? And if birthdays or holidays are too far away, you can use this same technique to make book coverings for school. Now you can make book covers with little pictures of your pets or make wrapping paper with the faces of all your family members on it!

For the best, most useful wrapping paper or book covers, it helps to be able to make bigger-than-average printouts on your inkjet printer. If all you can print is 8×10-inch paper, that's okay, but you'll only be wrapping small gifts or paperback books. A wide-format printer that can make 13×19-inch prints is better. No matter what kind of printer you have, try this:

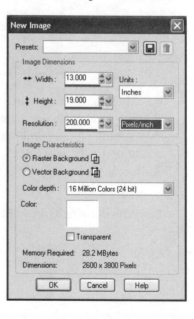

1. In an image editing program like Paint Shop Pro, create a new, blank picture. Choose File | New and, in the New Image dialog, specify a print size. If your printer supports such a size, choose 13×19 inches and 200 pixels/inch, as in the following image. If not, set the dimensions to 8×10 inches and 200 pixels/inch. Then click OK.

2. In the Materials palette on the right side of the screen, pick the color that you want your paper to be by clicking with the left mouse button in the color palette.

3. Click the Flood Fill tool—the fifth from the bottom of the tools palette on the left side of the screen. Then click the Flood Fill in the blank canvas.

4. Now we'll add pictures onto the paper-like little stickers. Open an image that you want to apply to the paper.

5. Now we'll resize the new picture so it'll be fairly small on the sheet of paper. Choose Image | Resize and set the picture dimensions to about 600 or 800 pixels wide. Click OK to make the change.

6. Now grab the Selection tool (it lives in the fifth cubby from the top of the tool palette) and set the selection type to rectangle. For a cool effect around the edges of the picture, set the Feather to about 50 pixels. Select most of the picture and choose Edit | Copy from the menu.

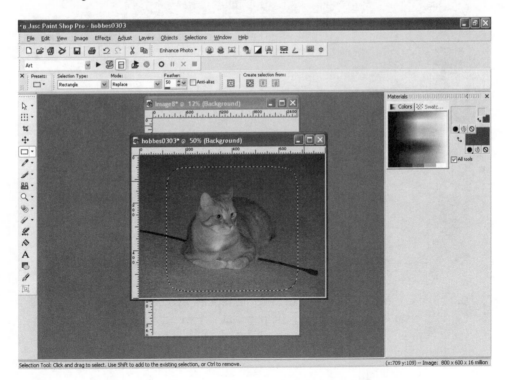

7. Now it's time to stick the picture in our wrapping paper. Switch to the sheet of colored paper and choose Edit | Paste | As New Selection. Click on the page where you want the image to appear.

8. Ready for the cool part? You can spin it so the picture appears at some random angle instead of being perfectly square with the rest of the paper. Click the Deform tool (in the second cubby from the top) and select the picture you just pasted. You might have to click OK to promote the picture to a layer—don't worry about this; just click OK. Click on the rotate handle of the picture (in the middle on the right edge of the picture) and spin the picture until it looks good to you.

9. Now it's just a matter of lather, rinse, repeat—you can paste many copies of the same picture all over the paper at any weird angle you like, or you can mix it up and make the paper out of a bunch of different pictures. It's up to you. You can see a sample sheet in Figure 10-2.

When you're done, just print the paper and use it to wrap up anything you like.

FIGURE 10-2   Make your own gift wrap with some digital photos and an inkjet printer.

Make Photo Letterhead in Microsoft Word

If you use Microsoft Word and send a lot of letters, you might want to try this next project—creating your own personal letterhead with an embedded digital image. Here's what to do:

1. Open Microsoft Word. If you don't already have a new blank document open, click the New Document icon in the toolbar.

2. Design the letterhead any way you like. You should set your formatting to single space and try to keep your text smaller than about 11 points.

3. To insert an image from your digital camera, choose Insert | Picture | From File and locate the image you want to include. The image will appear in your document.

4. To make the image easier to move around and position on the page, you need to put a frame around the picture. Right-click the image and choose Format Picture.

5. Click on the Layout tab and choose Tight.

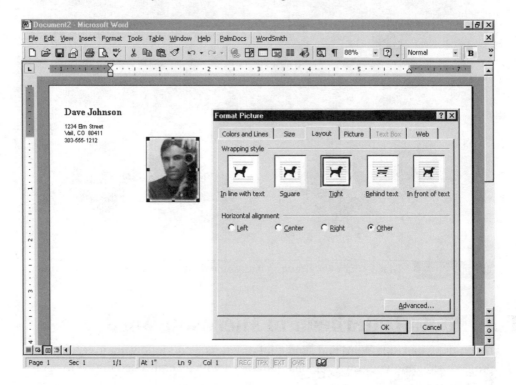

6. Click OK.

7. Position the image in the letterhead region of your document, such as to the left of your name. Notice how the text moves to accommodate the image.

8. Finish the letterhead by drawing a thin horizontal line under the text and image (see Figure 10-3). To do that, activate the drawing tools by clicking the Drawing icon in the toolbar. Then click the Line tool and drag out a horizontal line, holding down the SHIFT key at the same time. The line will snap to the horizontal automatically.

Document2 - Microsoft Word

File Edit View Insert Format Tools Table Window Help PalmDocs WordSmith

Dave Johnson

1234 Elm Street
Vail, CO 80411
303-555-1212

dave@bydavejohnson.com
www.bydavejohnson.com

Draw ▼   AutoShapes ▼

Page 1   Sec 1   1/1   At 1"   Ln 9   Col 1   REC TRK EX

10

FIGURE 10-3   Images can make your letterhead quite elegant.

Conduct a Mystery Photo Contest

Kids never seem to run out of cool things to take pictures of. But if your kids need some inspiration, suggest that they conduct their own Mystery Photo Contest. It could become a weekly event in your household!

What is a Mystery Photo Contest, you ask? Picture this:

What is it? That's the contest. Armed with a camera, your kids can sniff out ordinary objects in the house and around the neighborhood. When taken close-up, many of these things take on weird and otherworldly appearances—especially if they're shown upside down or at an unexpected angle. If you don't want to entrust your kids with an expensive digital camera, don't forget that you can also send them off to shoot pictures with a cheap disposable film camera. Shutterfly can even develop those picture and send you the prints!

By the way: the previous illustration is the tip of a container of white glue. Did you guess it? Maybe you're ready to be a contestant at your family's next Mystery Photo Contest.

Create Your Own Greeting Cards

You can make greeting cards using your computer any way you like: the super-easy way, the fairly easy way, and the not-as-easy-but-still-not-very-hard way. The easiest way is by turning your favorite photos into greeting cards at Shutterfly—see the next section for details. Or, you can use one of the many greeting card software packages on the market (see Figure 10-4). Not only can you import your digital camera images into these programs, but they also come with a considerable collection of clip art and premade card templates.

If you don't have one of those programs, you can still make your own greeting cards in a page layout program or Microsoft Word—consider it your backup plan if you need to make a birthday card for a party that's happening *this afternoon* and you only have a few minutes to put something together. Almost everyone has Microsoft Word—let's create a card in that. Before we get started, though, it's worth pointing out that you can make a greeting card on the PC using two common methods: the single-fold and the dual-fold.

Single-fold cards are simply made from 8.5×11-inch paper or cardstock and folded once down the middle, so the card measures 5.5×8.5 inches. This is a slightly oversized card, but it's a good size and the one we usually use. The alternative is a dual-fold card that's folded once lengthwise and again widthwise, for a card that measures 5.5×4.25 inches. The disadvantage to this kind of card is it's a bit small and it has a potentially amateurish double-fold along one edge (see Figure 10-5).

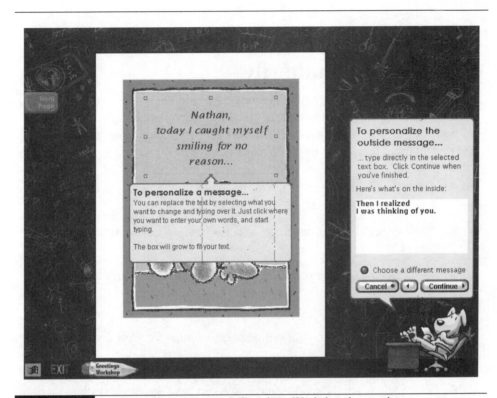

FIGURE 10-4   Programs like Microsoft Greetings Workshop let you import your own digital images into their greeting card templates.

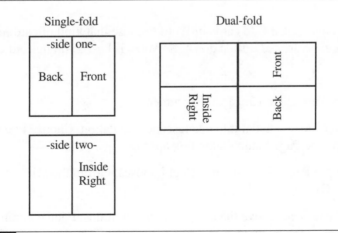

FIGURE 10-5   You can make either single-fold or dual-fold cards on your PC with almost any program.

How to ...   **Make a Greeting Card on Shutterfly**

Shutterfly's professionally printed greeting cards are the best way to turn your personal pictures into cards—the cards look like they were bought in a store instead of printed on your home printer, and yet they include your own photos and personalized text. Here's how to make one:

1. Click the Shutterfly Store tab at the top of the Shutterfly web page. Click Cards on the left side of the screen.

2. Click the card style you like—such as Greeting Cards, 4×8 Cards, or Note Cards.

3. Pick the type of card you want to make, for instance Party Invitation, Thank You Card, or Baby Announcement. A wide range of seasonal choices is also available.

4. Pick any image from your online photo albums for your card.

5. Finish the card by adding a greeting inside the card and click Next.

6. When you reach the mailing page, you can have the entire stack of cards mailed to you or you can have Shutterfly mail the cards for you. Just enter the addresses you want to send them to and Shutterfly does the rest.

You can't make dual-fold cards in Word because that kind of card requires one of the panels to be printed upside down. So Word is best at single-fold cards, as in this example:

1. Open Word and create a new document.

2. Change the document into a landscape orientation. Choose File | Page Setup. The Page Setup dialog box appears.

3. Click the Paper Size tab and select Landscape from the orientation section. Click OK.

4. Now you need to give the document two columns. Each column will be a panel on the finished card. Choose Format | Columns.

5. In the Columns dialog box, select Two and click OK.

6. Now you can enter your text. The left column on the first page is the rear of the card. If you want to, you can add something to the bottom of the rear panel like commercial greeting cards have. Press ENTER enough times to get to the bottom of the page.

7. Now it's time for the front of the card. That's the right column on the first page, so press ENTER to get there. You'll probably want to insert an image there using Insert | Picture | From File. You can place text above or below the image, or you can integrate the text in the image in a program like Paint Shop Pro first. Be sure to experiment with large and stylish fonts for this card.

Microsoft's WordArt is a cool way to dress up a greeting card in Word. Choose Insert | Picture | WordArt to insert WordArt into your project. WordArt lets you turn plain text into a fancy 3-D piece of art, as seen in Figure 10-6.

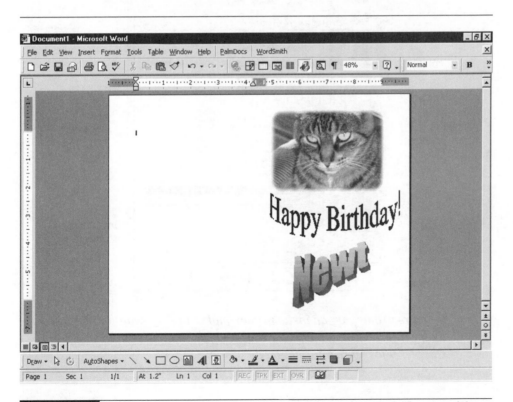

10

 Word can be used to make quick and dirty greeting cards if you need them immediately, though Shutterfly can offer you a more professional look.

8. The inside of the card is on the second page. The left inside panel is the left column, and the right inside panel is the right column. Enter text and images as necessary to lay out the card you want to create.

9. When you're done, you need to print your card manually so it doesn't print the second page of the document on a second sheet of paper. To do that, you have two choices:

   ■ Only load a single sheet of paper in the printer. When the first page is printed, turn the paper over and load it back in for the second pass, *or*

   ■ Change the printer settings. In Word, choose File | Print. Choose Properties to open the Printer Properties dialog box and change the printer's paper source to Manual Feed (your printer's dialog box might not look exactly like this one):

If you're printing on an inkjet printer, make sure you wait for the first side to dry before turning the paper over and printing the second side. See Chapter 9 for more information on printing.

TIP

Make a Photo Jigsaw Puzzle

When is a digital photo also a game the whole family can play? When it's a jigsaw puzzle. If you're looking for a new and unique activity for the family, consider turning pictures the family takes into jigsaw puzzles—which you can then solve together, or give to the kids to solve on their own. You can make pictures into real, live puzzles by gluing a print of your photo onto a piece of cardboard (the thicker the better) and then cutting it carefully into curved pieces.

If you're not that handy with glue and scissors, you can solve your puzzles on the computer screen. A number of computer games let you turn your own digital photos into jigsaw puzzles. Consider BrainsBreaker, for instance; it's an onscreen jigsaw puzzle game that lets you create puzzles out of any picture on your computer.

BrainsBreaker lets you import a photo, crop it down to just the part you want to turn into a puzzle, and select the number of and shape of your puzzle pieces. Then the desktop turns into the digital equivalent of your dining room table, complete with puzzle pieces lining the screen edges, a clear work area, and even a slew of "boxes" for storing pieces you don't need to work with right away.

You can download a free trial of BrainsBreaker at www.brainsbreaker.com. If you like it, the complete program costs $20.

Make a Photo Journal

There's a little reporter in every kid, or so it seems. If you want to nurture that aspect of your child's intellect, suggest that they create a Photo Journal. Here's how it works: your kid picks one day each week to carry a small digital camera around and snap pictures of anything interesting. There's just one rule: take pictures.

When the camera comes home at the end of the day, you and your child can transfer the pictures to the PC, and then organize the images into a journal, complete with captions for each picture. If you use Shutterfly, your kid can create an album and add those captions easily right on the Web without ever using an image editing program. You can even turn these photo journals into printed, bound albums at Shutterfly. These are ideal projects for Shutterfly Snapbooks and Photo Books!

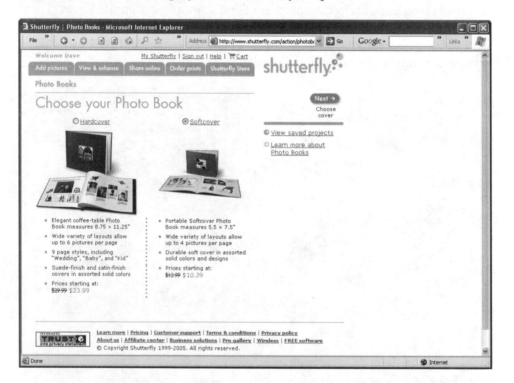

There's an added benefit to the Photo Journal—not only does your child have fun, but you get glimpses into his or her day that you can keep and look back on for years to come.

Create a Photo Collage

Why make a collage? Because it's fun—fun to make, fun to give, and fun to get. People have been making custom photo collages for eons—long before computers came along. There are all sorts of ways to make a collage, but this particular technique makes the photos look like they've been torn right out of a photo album. You can go a step further and add captions, too.

1. Start by creating a blank page in a program like Paint Shop Pro by choosing File | New. Enter the dimensions in the New Image dialog box. Because you'll probably want to print this as an 8×10-inch photo, change the units to inches, and enter **8** for width and **10** for height (or the other way around, depending on how you plan to orient the page). Set the resolution to **200** (that's a good resolution to print using most ink jet printers). Click OK. We'll come back to this blank page later.

2. Now it's time to start assembling photos. Paint Shop Pro makes it easy to see all the photos in a single folder at a glance: Choose File | Browse and use the folder list on the left to locate the pictures you want.

3. When you find your first photo, double-click it so that photo opens in Paint Shop Pro's work area.

4. Now it's time to crop the picture down to size. This is the cool part of the collage: instead of using a bunch of rectangular photos, you're going to cut them up so that they look like you trimmed them with scissors. Click the Freehand selection button in the toolbar (it looks like a lasso). Next, make sure it's set to Freehand mode in the Tool Options dialog box at the top of the screen. Now click, hold down the mouse button, and drag the pointer around the part of the image that you want to put in the collage. Complete the crop by encircling the image. Either end the trace near where you started it, letting the program finish the loop, or drag over the trace line from the outside of the crop, letting the program remove any "cuts" inside the crop. Don't worry if your lines looked jagged—you want things to look hand-done.

5. Next, choose Selections | Modify | Feather and set the Feather Value to about **5** pixels, and then click OK. This will create a slight blend effect so the edge of the picture blurs into the background.

6. Choose Edit | Copy, and then close the photo you just clipped because you don't need it anymore. Click the blank image you created in the first step and choose Edit | Paste | As New Layer. The cropped photo will appear in the scene. Click the Move Tool in the toolbar, and then drag your image around until it's more or less where you'd like it.

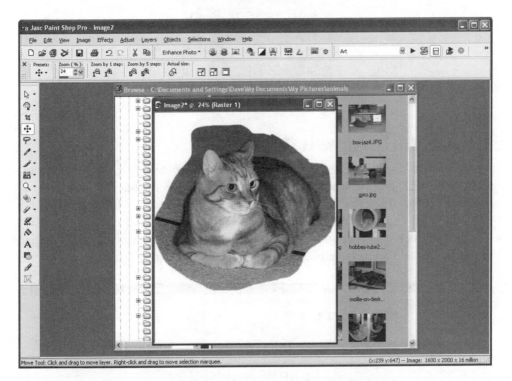

7. Is the picture too big or too small? You can resize the image you've just pasted into your collage page. Choose Image | Resize and change the first drop-down menu to Percent. Also be sure to uncheck the Resize All Layers option at the bottom of the dialog box. Then set a percentage to resize the picture and click OK. When you add another picture, it will be easily resizable as well.

8. Next, it's a simple case of lather, rinse, and repeat. Just return to the Browse window, drag another picture into a blank spot on your Paint Shop Pro screen, and then edit, crop, paste, and resize it in your collage screen. Do this for every picture you want to add to the collage.

That's all there is to it. When you're done, save the file and print your collage (shown on the next page).

Create a Family Newsletter

Equipped with Microsoft *Publisher* or a similar page layout program, you can create professional and attractive newsletters for your family, office, or club. Publisher comes in most versions of Microsoft Office, and we highly recommend it for making your own newsletters easily. Publisher is a wizard-based program. All you have to do is follow the directions to set up the overall look and feel of your document, and then fill in the text and replace the placeholder images with your own pictures.

How to ... **Create a Custom Calendar on Shutterfly**

A calendar lets you enjoy your best pictures year-round. And they make great gifts for everyone on your holiday list. All you need is your favorite pictures of the year (or of all times!) and a few words to describe them, and you can make a truly personalized gift that is memorable and affordable (many 12-month calendars are $19.99).

Shutterfly calendars are available in both 12- and 18-month formats. You can start the calendar on any month you want, giving you the flexibility of making special school-year themes or a timely birthday gift. Made of heavy card stock, the calendars will stand up to wear and tear and provide you with plenty of room for notes and the 8×10 photo-pages can even be framed at the end of the year. Here's how to make one:

1. Click the Shutterfly Store tab at the top of the Shutterfly web page.

2. Click Calendars on the left side of the screen.

3. Choose a starting month (for example, January), and then decide on either a 12-month or 18-month calendar format.

4. Pick your favorite images from your online photo albums, assign one picture to each month and then designate a cover image.

5. Personalize your calendar by adding border styles and captions or by changing a color picture to black-and-white.

6. Preview your calendar and when you're finished, choose the recipient (yourself or send it to friends or family members directly).

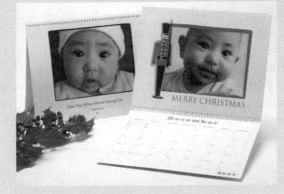

10

Make a Magazine Cover

At gift time, photos are some of the most personal and most appreciated gifts you can give. But just handing someone an 8×10 photo can sometimes lack that certain *je ne sais quois,* as the French like to say. So we like to do things with pictures that are a bit unusual. The next time a birthday rolls around, here's a clever gift you can make all by yourself: a framed mock magazine cover featuring your guest of honor.

This is easy to do. All you need is an appropriate, high-resolution photo and an image editing program to make some surgical changes. Then send it to the printer and it's ready for framing. Because this will eventually be printed on an ink jet printer at 8×10 size, you should start with a 2- or 3-megapixel image. For our example, we'll make the debut issue of *Kristen* magazine using this image:

1. Our first order of business is to give our picture a magazine-like outline. Load it into your image editor and add a blank border area around your image. You can make it any color you like but, for this picture, we think a nice fire-red border will be very magazine-ish. In Paint Shop Pro, there's

an easy way to do this. Choose Image | Add Borders, and then choose a color from the color box in the Add Borders dialog box. Next, enter a border dimension. If you're using a 3-megapixel image, you might need about **100** pixels of border to get the right effect, but experiment until you see something you like. Be sure to set the border to symmetric, so all four sides are the same. Click OK to create the border. You should see a red border added around the outside of the image.

2. What's a magazine without a catchy title? This one will be called *Kristen* magazine. After all: it's the place people go when they want to read all about Kris. Click the Text button and adjust the font style, size, and color. Set the Create as to Vector. Click in the upper half of the picture, more or less where the title should end up. You'll then get the Text Entry dialog box. Type a title, and then select it with your cursor, drag the text around the screen, and even change its size. If you want to get fancy, you can even rotate it by clicking-and-dragging the small box to the right of the center of the text.

3. From here, it's all up to you. Add some "cover lines" to your magazine to make it look more like a real publication. Add an issue date, some revealing new feature, and more. If you're ambitious, you can photograph a bar code from a real magazine with your digital camera and paste it into the cover. Our first draft looks something like this:

Shake Hands with Elvis

If you aren't on a first name basis with Arnold Schwarzenegger or Madonna, here's a chance to get a picture of your wife, dad, or son in a scene with one of those celebrities anyway. It's not really all that hard. Let's suppose that your friend, Kristen, has always wanted to meet Elvis. Sadly, it's too late to set up a meeting, but you can do the next best thing. In the following steps, we'll combine a picture of Kristen with an old shot from the Nixon administration (to see the finished product, check out Figure 10-7).

1. First, you need a suitable picture of Kristen—one in which she's more or less the same size as Elvis. Load the picture of the King into Paint Shop Pro and choose Image | Image Information to find out how tall Elvis is in the selected image.

2. Armed with knowledge about Elvis, load the picture of Kristen and crop her so that she's only seen from the waist up—like Elvis—and resize the image, using the Image | Resize menu, until she's about the right height.

3. Now for a little housecleaning. You need to erase as much of Nixon as you reasonably can, perhaps using the Clone tool. In this case, we copied the flag to Elvis's immediate left over the flag that was directly behind Nixon, and then copied the surrounding wall to get rid of as much of the former president as possible. It isn't essential to erase all of him, because we're going to position Kristen over part of this image. This is what it looked like when the image was getting close to good enough to paste in Kris:

4. Now for the tricky part. You need to use a selection tool to copy
    Kristen, but avoid including any of the background. You can use
    the Magic Wand, Freehand tool—whichever you're most comfortable
    with. Try the Smart Edge tool, which often gives fairly good results in
    situations like this.

5. Once she's selected, it becomes obvious that the transition from Kristen to
    the background is too sharp to be believable. That means it won't look realistic
    in the final picture. Use the Feather tool to smooth out the edges of the
    selected region. Choose Selections | Modify | Feather and choose a value
    of about **4** pixels.

6. Copy Kristen to the clipboard, and then switch to the other image. Choose
    Paste | As New Layer. She'll appear onstage next to Elvis.

7. Position her in the new image, arranging her so their hands meet, as shown
    in Figure 10-7.

FIGURE 10-7   You—or your kids—can now shake hands with Elvis.

8. There's something a bit squirrelly about their handshake. If you arrange the image so that Elvis's arm appears over Kristen, you can mask her badly cropped appendage with a bit of Nixon's leftover hand and create a slightly three-dimensional effect—she's in front of his left shoulder but behind his arm. To do that, copy Elvis's arm to the clipboard and paste it back into the image as a new layer, exactly over the old arm. The only difference is that it'll end up lying over Kristen's hand, making it look more like they're in the same picture.

To make the illusion more convincing, you can try to sharpen or blur Kristen a bit to match the original Elvis photo before you copy and paste her. The CIA might know it's a fake, but it's probably fine for putting on a birthday card or framing for a gag gift.

Put Your Kid in a Jar

Have you ever been impressed by the fanciful digital art in magazine ads that depict the impossible or the far, far-fetched? We can't promise that you will soon be able to photograph a cow driving your car or aliens posing with your dog while it plays the piano, but let us show you how easy it is to do something both cute and clever— we'll put your kid in an old mayonnaise jar. Hopefully, when you see how easy it is to pull this stunt off, you'll want to make up a few clever gags of your own.

Actually, this is going to be easy. We'll take a few pictures and combine them in layers within Paint Shop Pro, resizing them to achieve the effect we want. Do this:

1. Start by finding a nice, big jar (when we made this shot, we used a clear plastic peanut butter jar. But a mayo jar or any large, clear container is ideal). Photograph someone peering inquisitively into it.

2. Next, take one of your kids and pose them in front of a big backdrop. Ideally, you can shoot them against a plain wall that's all one color, but if not, just shoot the picture outdoors and we'll deal with it.

3. Load the two images into Paint Shop Pro, but bring your trapped kid to the front—we'll work with this picture first.

4. If you managed to photograph the subject in front of a solid background, it'll be easier. Use the Magic Wand tool until the entire background is selected, leaving just the kid. Using a subtle feathering in the Tool Options dialog box will help you out later.

5. When the background is entirely selected, choose Selections | Invert from the menu.

TIP

If you have a very irregular background to contend with, you might want to use the Background Eraser or SmartEdge selection tool instead of the Magic Wand.

6. Once the subject is selected, copy it to the clipboard by choosing Edit | Copy from the menu.

7. Bring the jar photograph to the front and choose Edit | Paste | As New Layer from the menu. Your kid should appear onscreen in the photo.

Now it's time to shrink the new addition down to size. Choose Image | Resize from the menu. In the Resize dialog box, remove the check mark from Resize All Layers (it's near the bottom). In the Percent of Original box, enter a number that you think will reduce the subject to fit in the jar. Try, for instance, **20 percent**.

8. Click on the subject and drag it on top of the jar. If it fits, fine. If not, return to the Resize dialog box and fine-tune its size until it fits properly in the jar.

Once you tweak the size and position of the captured kid, your photo is done, as you can see in Figure 10-8. You can try other things, though, to improve the photo.

■ Try to photograph both pictures with similar lighting to make a more believable picture.

■ Be careful about the angle from which you shoot the jar-kid to match the jar's perspective in the first photo.

■ Select the jar, copy it to the clipboard, and paste it on top of the kid as yet another layer to increase the illusion that the subject is indeed inside the jar, not just pasted on top of it.

FIGURE 10-8   You can put your kid in an old mayo jar with about ten minutes of editing.

Index

INTERNATIONAL CONTACT INFORMATION

AUSTRALIA
McGraw-Hill Book Company
Australia Pty. Ltd.
TEL +61-2-9900-1800
FAX +61-2-9878-8881
http://www.mcgraw-hill.com.au
books-it_sydney@mcgraw-hill.com

CANADA
McGraw-Hill Ryerson Ltd.
TEL +905-430-5000
FAX +905-430-5020
http://www.mcgraw-hill.ca

**GREECE, MIDDLE EAST, & AFRICA
(Excluding South Africa)**
McGraw-Hill Hellas
TEL +30-210-6560-990
TEL +30-210-6560-993
TEL +30-210-6560-994
FAX +30-210-6545-525

MEXICO (Also serving Latin America)
McGraw-Hill Interamericana Editores
S.A. de C.V.
TEL +525-1500-5108
FAX +525-117-1589
http://www.mcgraw-hill.com.mx
carlos_ruiz@mcgraw-hill.com

SINGAPORE (Serving Asia)
McGraw-Hill Book Company
TEL +65-6863-1580
FAX +65-6862-3354
http://www.mcgraw-hill.com.sg
mghasia@mcgraw-hill.com

SOUTH AFRICA
McGraw-Hill South Africa
TEL +27-11-622-7512
FAX +27-11-622-9045
robyn_swanepoel@mcgraw-hill.com

SPAIN
McGraw-Hill/
Interamericana de España, S.A.U.
TEL +34-91-180-3000
FAX +34-91-372-8513
http://www.mcgraw-hill.es
professional@mcgraw-hill.es

**UNITED KINGDOM, NORTHERN,
EASTERN, & CENTRAL EUROPE**
McGraw-Hill Education Europe
TEL +44-1-628-502500
FAX +44-1-628-770224
http://www.mcgraw-hill.co.uk
emea_queries@mcgraw-hill.com

ALL OTHER INQUIRIES Contact:
McGraw-Hill/Osborne
TEL +1-510-420-7700
FAX +1-510-420-7703
http://www.osborne.com
omg_international@mcgraw-hill.com